The
POACHER'S
MOON

A true story of life, death, love and survival in Africa

Richard Peirce

Published by Struik Nature (an imprint of
Random House Struik (Pty) Ltd)
Reg. No. 1966/003153/07
The Estuaries No. 4, Oxbow Crescent, Century
Avenue, Century City, 7441
PO Box 1144, Cape Town, 8000 South Africa

Visit **www.randomstruik.co.za** and join the
Struik Nature Club for updates, news, events
and special offers.

First published in 2013 by Shark Cornwall,
Dulverton House, Crooklets, Bude,
Cornwall, EX23 8NE, United Kingdom

New edition published in 2014 by Struik Nature

10 9 8 7 6 5 4 3 2 1

Copyright © in text, 2013, 2014: Richard Peirce
Copyright © in photographs, 2013, 2014: Jacqui
Peirce or as indicated under 'Picture credits'
Copyright © in map, 2014: MapStudio 2014
Copyright © in published edition, 2014:
Random House Struik (Pty) Ltd

Publisher: Pippa Parker
Editor: Helen de Villiers
Designer: Janice Evans

Reproduction by Hirt & Carter
Cape (Pty) Ltd
Printed and bound by Interpak Books,
Pietermaritzburg

ISBN   978-1-77584-178-4
ePub   978-1-77584-179-1
PDF   978-1-77584-180-7

PICTURE CREDITS

Covers: Joe Hilley (front); Mario Moreno/South
Cape Images (back)
Inside pages: Anne Albert: 95 (top), 104–105
(various); Aquila Private Game Reserve: 18, 20
(inset left & main image), 21, 24, 25, 26–27, 29;
Egmont Strigl/Imagebroker/FLPA: 135; Eugene
Braun: illustration, 3; Fairy Glen Private Game
Reserve: 12–13, 14, 17, 33, 37 (x3), 38, 39, 40
(x3), 41 (top), 42–43, 44, 46, 47, 49 (x2), 53
(x2), 54, 76 (x2), 84–85, 134; Gerard Scholtz:
92, 94 (x3), 95 (middle), 104–105 (various);
Independent Newspapers: 78, 128, 137 (bottom)
– collated by Anne Albert; Inverdoorn Game
Reserve: 10–11, 62 (top), 70, 71, 133 (bottom);
Jim Brandenburg/Minden Pictures/FLPA: 122;
John P Seely: 124–125; Julian Rademeyer/
KillingforProfit.com: 119 (top); Lanz von
Hörsten/Images of Africa: 112–113; Linda Piegl:
119 (bottom); Nick Burdett: 138; Roger de la
Harpe/Images of Africa: 7; Wikimedia CC BY
2.0: 127; Wikimedia CC BY-SA 3.0: 125 (inset)

DEDICATION

This book is dedicated to Higgins and Lady and to all the
rhinos, dead and alive, that have been attacked by poachers.
It is also dedicated to the brave men and women who work on
the front line trying to protect animals – some of whom have
been killed doing their jobs. We owe it to the human and rhino
victims to develop effective conservation measures to ensure
the survival of the remaining rhino species in the wild.

Contents

Forewords

ALL TRADE IS BASED ON SUPPLY AND DEMAND. When there is a demand there will always be a supply. Prohibition in the USA, the global drugs trade, and human trafficking, etc., all had, and have, massive and sophisticated police resources deployed against them, but the supply has continued and often increased.

The trade in wildlife and animal body parts is no different. Rhino horn, ivory, shark fins, and others continue to be harvested legally and illegally to satisfy an ever growing demand. The lessons of history indicate that we will not save Earth's wildlife by trying to regulate or stop supply. The only thing that will ultimately prove effective is to regulate demand.

The conservation of our wild fauna and flora rests on a highly complex set of issues. However, for many animal species the demand comes from a limited part of the world, and to a large degree from one country within that area – China. If conservation NGOs, CITES, the IUCN and others turned their attention to stopping demand, rather than tinkering with supply, their efforts would be more effective. Humans have always hunted wild animals and eaten parts of them. However, the difference today is that many of these species face extinction, and often consumption is based on ancient beliefs, reinforced by spurious medical claims. This mistaken belief and the fact that targeted species may now face extinction in the wild constitute powerful arguments; the global conservation community should deploy them in Southeast Asia to stop the demand.

Jacqui Peirce

4

HACKING BODY PARTS OFF LIVING ANIMALS for calculated financial gain places humans in a behavioural class on their own at the bottom of the pile.

Every year millions of sharks have their fins cut off while they're still alive, rhinos are darted and immobilised while their horns are hacked off, bears have catheters inserted into their gall bladders to remove bile, and the list goes on …

In 2013, 1,004 rhinos were poached in South Africa, and I have often heard the struggle against poaching referred to as a war. The rangers, park wardens, police and military fighting the poachers cannot win the war as long as the value of rhino horn is so high that people are prepared to risk their lives to acquire it. What makes the war even more uneven is that the poachers can make the rules up as they go along, while those on the other side have to play by the book.

Rhinos have been on our planet for around 50 million years; by comparison, humans have been on Earth for 10 minutes. If humans continue to live unsustainably, then perhaps they will wipe themselves out before they succeed in eliminating the rhino, which may just be around in another 50 million years, long after humans have disappeared!

The Poacher's Moon is the story of rhino poaching on three game farms in South Africa's Western Cape. It is my tribute to those who fight to safeguard the targeted, vulnerable species on our planet, and to Higgins and Lady – two rhinos that have survived the slaughter to see another dawn.

Richard Peirce

RICHARD PEIRCE

Acknowledgements

I WOULD LIKE TO THANK THE FOLLOWING for their help in turning *The Poacher's Moon* from a story that I wanted to write into a reality:

Anne Albert; Lawrence Anthony (author of *The Last Rhinos*); Johan Botma, Denis Pothas, Deon and Chantelle from Fairy Glen; Eugene Braun for the original front cover illustration, now appearing on page 3; Wilfred Chivell and Brenda du Toit for help and advice on legal issues; Rudi Coertzen and Gerard Scholtz for their excellent camera work; Trevor Carnaby (author of *Beat About The Bush*); Tim Davison who edited the original manuscript; Searl Derman, Mandi Jarman and the staff at the Aquila Game Reserve; Denise Headon and Madelein Marais who made up for my keyboard ineptitude; Damien Vergnaud, Wilna Paxton and the staff at the Inverdoorn Game Reserve; Esmond Bradley Martin, Gerard Scholtz, Dr Gerhard Steenkamp; Clive and Anton Walker (authors of *The Rhino Keepers*).

Special thanks must go to Pieter de Jager, the owner of the Fairy Glen Reserve, who gave unstintingly of his time to help me, and Dr Jana Pretorius who was kind enough to read the book, even though I know it upset her, to give me a factual check.

Chapter 9 draws heavily on *Killing for Profit*, which is an excellent work by Julian Rademeyer. *The Poacher's Moon* is the story of two animals that survived attacks in the Western Cape, and others who didn't. For the serious student of rhino poaching I unreservedly recommend Rademeyer's book.

Finally a huge thank you to my wife Jacqui who took lots of the photographs and worked with me on many aspects of the book.

RHINOS WHITE AND BLACK

There are two types of rhinoceros in southern Africa: the square-lipped or white rhinoceros (*Ceratotherium simum*), as seen below, and the hook-lipped or black rhinoceros (*Diceros bicornis*). From their earlier widespread occurrence across Africa, both white and black rhinos' numbers have been severely impacted by poaching and they are now restricted to a fraction of their original distribution, mostly on game reserves. This account deals principally with rhinos re-introduced to three game reserves in the Western Cape, and all are white rhinos.

RHINO FACTS

- There are five rhino species: the Indian, Sumatran (the smallest), Javan, and African black and white rhinos.
- The last rhino in southern Java was shot in 1934; however, 20–40 animals remain in West Java.
- The last captive Javan rhino died in Adelaide Zoo in 1907.
- The name rhinoceros comes from the Greek *rhino* (nose) and *ceros* (horn).
- A group of rhinos is called a crash.
- Rhinos have been on planet Earth for over 50 million years.
- The white rhino is the second largest land species after the elephant.
- Rhinos are related to horses and zebras.
- Depending on the species, rhinos live for between 30 and 60 years.
- White rhinos have a shoulder height of up to 1.8m.
- White rhinos can weigh up to approximately 3,000kg.
- White rhinos can run at speeds of up to 40km per hour.
- Rhinos leave piles of dung as messages for other rhinos.
- Rhinos are herbivores (vegetarians).
- The gestation period for rhinos is 15–16 months.
- White rhino calves weigh 45–65kg at birth.
- Rhino horn is made of keratin.
- Rhino horn will regrow at a rate of 6–10cm per annum.
- Rhino horn is now worth more than gold at over $65,000 per kilogram.
- Humans are the rhino's most dangerous predators.

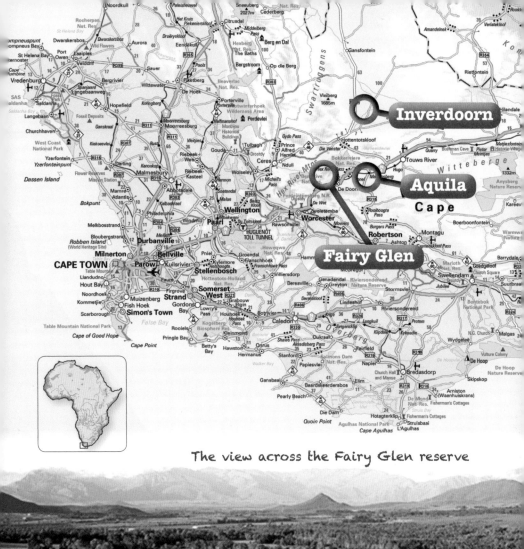

Inverdoorn

Aquila
Cape

Fairy Glen

The view across the Fairy Glen reserve

PART ONE

1

Limpopo dawn, life begins

Small smoke-like puffs of dust rose from the ground with every footfall as the huge, grey, prehistoric-looking creature made its way silently across the moonlit African landscape.

Higgins and Lady graze contentedly before the attack.

The female southern white rhino was 16 months pregnant and ready to give birth. She had a rounded look to her and her belly swung slightly as she walked. Her calf would weigh only 45–65kg, so even at full term it would be a relatively small foetus compared to its mother's massive three-ton bulk.

The moon cast a perfect shadow of her as she walked slowly across the flat sandy area, heading for the cover of some trees and bushes a couple of hundred metres away. At the front of the shadow were two magnificent horns that rose to sharp points. It was a full moon, sometimes known as a 'poacher's moon', and later on, just such a moon would play a major part in the life of her new calf.

A week ago, after chasing off her two-year-old calf in preparation for the new arrival, the cow rhino had left her crash (group of

rhinos) and gone in search of a quiet place to give birth. She pushed the branches aside with her horn, and walked in and out of the moonlight, making her way through the shadows cast by the bushes and trees. She entered a small area of clear ground that had a slight depression in one corner. She circled the little clearing, stopping often to listen and sniff the air. Apparently satisfied, she lay down in the shallow depression, found a lump of wood and amused herself chewing it while she waited.

Two hours later, lying on her side, she gave birth to a 50kg male calf, which arrived with a wet, squelchy, gurgling sound. The baby southern white rhino, which would one day become world famous and be known as Higgins, had made his undignified entry into the world. Higgins was standing on his wobbly legs within an hour and was soon trying to suckle. His was an experienced mother who helped manoeuvre him into position, and by the time he was two hours old he was steady on his legs and feeding contentedly.

For the next two months Higgins and his mother were rarely more than a few feet apart, and very often he was in front of his mother

Higgins and Lady quickly become inseparable companions.

and appeared to be leading the way. Higgins started grazing at three months and by then mother and calf were often in the company of other rhinos in their crash.

At the time of Higgins' birth in 2000 the population of southern white rhino had recovered from near extinction. There were only a few hundred of them in 1900, rising to about 19,000 in the year 2000, mostly in South Africa. Higgins was born in the north of South Africa's Limpopo province, only a few kilometres from the border with Botswana.

Four years later, in the southern Kruger National Park, a female calf was born whose life would eventually become entwined with that of Higgins and who would also become an unwitting global celebrity. She would later be known as Lady and, coincidentally, she was also born under a full moon.

When Higgins was five years old he was loaded into a specially adapted truck and, under the watchful eye of vet Jana Pretorius, was driven 1,500km to his new home on the Fairy Glen Private Game Reserve. He was happy enough in his new surroundings, but a single rhino looked strange and lonely and in 2010 Fairy Glen's owner, Pieter de Jager, bought a female companion for Higgins.

Lady, now aged six, arrived at the reserve in late 2010 and the pair quickly became inseparable. They grazed together, walked and mud bathed together, slept side by side, and a year after Lady had arrived they were seen mating.

The De Jager family had bought Fairy Glen in the early 1970s. The farm is overlooked by the Auden Mountain, which is part of the Brandwacht range and towers to a height of 1,624m (5,331ft) to the north of the main farm buildings. There is snow on the mountains in winter, and Fairy Glen was once a ski resort. Some of today's guest safari lodges are yesterday's converted ski chalets.

Fairy Glen's main gate

The farm was a vineyard when the De Jagers had bought it 40 years earlier, but it was not ideally suited to growing grapes. The family had made the farm viable by introducing mixed farming: they grazed sheep, reared cattle and grew crops until, in 2000, Pieter de Jager converted Fairy Glen into a game reserve and opened it to the public.

Pieter believes that the last white rhino in the Western Cape was shot and killed in 1691 on what is now Fairy Glen. The trigger was pulled by Simon van der Stel who was the first governor of the Cape Colony. If this story is true, there is a gap of 314 years until Higgins arrived and rhinos once again lived in the shadow of the Auden Mountain. Fairy Glen is a small reserve, which is largely covered by fynbos (natural shrubland), grass fields, scrub and some woodland. The Lodge is situated 2km up a track from the main gate and occupies a wonderful position overlooking the dam, which means that guests have an uninterrupted view of the animals as they come to drink. Despite its small size, Fairy Glen is home to 17 species, and the De Jagers hoped that their rhinos would breed and further add to the appeal of the reserve. But by the time Higgins and Lady began their life together at Fairy Glen in 2010, rhino poaching had once again become a scourge that was starting to threaten the survival of the species in the wild.

Rhinos rest in the shade during the hottest hours of the day; here Higgins and Lady take a nap, unaware of the trauma to come.

ABSA was something of a celebrity — the first
rhino reintroduced into the Western Cape since
their local extinction from hunting decades earlier.
Now he was fighting for his life.

2

Attack on Aquila

The Aquila Private Game Reserve lies just off the N1, 10km to the west of Touws River. It is a commercially successful reserve handling over 60,000 visitors a year – a mix of overnight guests and day trippers who are mainly tourists from Cape Town, which is less than two hours away by road.

The other game reserves that are within a couple of hours' drive from Cape Town are Fairy Glen and Inverdoorn. All three reserves can lay claim to being home to Africa's Big Five – elephant, rhino, lion, buffalo and leopard, although leopards occur infrequently and visitors are very lucky to see one. Of the Big Five species on the reserves, buffaloes, rhinos and leopards are free roaming, whereas elephants are sometimes kept in bomas and lions in small, separate, fenced reserves.

There are people who criticise such relatively small reserves and call them fenced farms or large zoos. However, the other side of the coin is that they give visitors an opportunity to see Africa's main game species only a short drive from the tourist magnet that is Cape Town. Most visitors don't have the time, opportunity or inclination to go to the Kruger or the Kgalagadi Transfrontier Park, or to drive to Etosha in Namibia, or the Okavango Delta in Botswana, and these smaller, tamer alternatives provide a taste of African wildlife.

The Aquila Private Game Reserve is the brainchild of owner Searl Derman and opened for business in 1999. The first rhino, a male, arrived in 2002 and was nicknamed ABSA after the bank that advanced the money to buy him. Further animals were acquired and, by August 2011, there were six rhinos on the reserve.

Above and opposite: The poachers must have been interrupted as ABSA is left with part of his horn intact.

Saturday 20 August 2011 began like any other day for Searl Derman when he woke at his home in Cape Town. Then, at 9.00 a.m. he answered a call on his cellphone and it suddenly felt as if the blood in his veins was freezing. A year earlier a lawyer friend of his from Johannesburg had warned him that the rhinos at Aquila were a target for poachers, so Searl already knew it was just a matter of time before his animals came under fire. Now the nightmare was happening: the call was from the reserve, to inform him that his rhinos had been attacked by poachers.

He had bought weapons and applied for licences, but the weapons remained in storage as the licences had not yet come through. Perhaps this was a blessing because, had his rangers been armed and come across the poachers, there would have been a firefight with the possibility of human deaths on both sides. There is evidence that the rangers did, albeit unwittingly, disturb the poachers who broke off their attack and fled.

Searl drove up the N1 towards Aquila as fast as he could. The news was that two rhinos were missing, and another was fighting for its life. He realised his two priorities were to try and save the injured rhino, and organise a search for the missing animals, which might also be injured or dead. He stopped in Paarl to try and pick up some antidote to the anaesthetic dart that would have been used, but couldn't find the right one. He phoned his vet who advised him to get the human equivalent, and he ended up jumping over a pharmacy counter, grabbing as much as he could, paying, and leaving to continue his dash to Aquila. The journey from hell hadn't finished because at some point he hit bumps going over the veld and the door of his vehicle locked, temporarily trapping him inside.

He reached the reserve just after 11.30 a.m. and walked into a maelstrom of activity that badly needed organising and directing. Vets had already arrived but they were small-animal vets with no experience of rhinos. ABSA, the male rhino, had had a horn hacked off and was stumbling around in a tormented daze. There were cuts on the second horn, but it was still on the animal with part of a saw blade broken off in the wound. This, and other evidence that would come to light later, pointed to the poachers having been disturbed during their raid.

Searl's first priority was to get the antidote into the rhino. ABSA was something of a celebrity as he was the first rhino reintroduced into the Western Cape since their local extinction from hunting decades earlier. Injecting antidote is a dangerous business even when the subject is half dazed and injured, as ABSA was. Searl awaited his chance and injected him in the rump. Despite having one injured leg, the rhino stayed on his feet. He quickly seemed brighter and hopes for his survival increased.

Searl now turned his attention to organising the search for the missing rhinos, hoping against hope that he wouldn't find them with their faces hacked off, bleeding and dying. Quad bikes, horses, vehicles and helicopters were all searching the veld for the missing animals. The first was found stumbling around in a wooded area. She was ABSA's daughter and had been darted but still had her horns, which was further evidence that the poachers had fled before finishing their work.

Searl kept her attention, allowing the vet to approach from behind and administer the antidote. Two animals had now been successfully injected with the antidote. One was injured and the other not, but there was nothing more Searl could do for either at the moment, so he took to a helicopter to search for the last missing rhino.

In due course they spotted a still, grey body lying in a gully with a pool of blood around its head and a pile of dung at its rear. With the syringe in his hand Searl leapt from the helicopter as soon as it touched down and sprinted to the inert grey mass. Even as he ran he knew he was too late: the rhino was dead, the huge amount of blood and the bowel evacuation being sure signs. The dead rhino was discovered just after 1.00 p.m., only four hours after Searl had received the call at his Cape Town home.

It was the guests on the early game drive who discovered the stricken ABSA, and raised the alarm that the reserve had been attacked. A vehicle full of ordinary tourists looking forward to seeing some of Africa's wildlife suddenly found themselves on the frontline of the war against poaching. The awful reality of rhino poaching is cruelty, suffering, blood and death, and the images the tourists saw that day will remain with them for a long time. They had seen what humans will do to other animals for money.

Searl had started with six rhinos – now one had been killed, one had been saved by the antidote, and one was critically ill. When ABSA had gone down after being darted he had collapsed on a rocky surface, lying awkwardly on one of his legs. Now, not only was half his face missing, but restricted blood circulation had damaged his leg, limiting his ability to move. This lack of mobility meant he couldn't easily regulate his body temperature by seeking shade or a mud bath if he got hot at midday, and at night he could get too cold if in an exposed place. Attempts to get him to drink from man-made puddles and buckets had been largely unsuccessful.

23

Searl Derman despairs as he mourns his rhino –

On day three, ABSA had to be darted again to get a fluid drip into him for a couple of hours. Afterwards, when giving the antidote, Searl nearly got into serious trouble. The quantity of fluid to be injected was large and the only syringe big enough was a plastic one. The vet had failed to get the drug in and Searl took over, making a last desperate attempt. He managed to inject most of the fluid, but then the syringe broke and the rest ended up in his face. For an instant Searl thought his days were up, but he kept calm, and dousing his face with a bucket of water saved the situation. Luckily he was still working with the human antidote – the rhino equivalent would inevitably have landed him in hospital.

and confronts the brutal reality of poaching.

ABSA managed to move short distances but was immobile most of the time. Crows sensed he was in trouble and came to peck at his eyes, and there were fears that, if he was left unattended, buffaloes, leopards and elephants would all pose threats.

Rhinos can make an almost human crying noise, and many times during these difficult days the sounds ABSA made brought tears to his carers' eyes. ABSA's daughter was distressed by her father's plight and tried to get near to comfort and lie down next to him. The presence of a fully fit, very troubled young rhino made the work of ABSA's carers even more dangerous: she tried to protect her father by preventing Searl and his team from getting close to him.

To win the battle for ABSA's life, Searl had to create an 'intensive care unit' in a protected zone to restrict ABSA's movement and prevent interference from other animals. He decided to use a big truck like an F250 or a Dodge with a large robust trailer, a crane and a cradle in case ABSA needed lifting, and ultrasound equipment to massage the injured leg. He brought in five 12m containers with which to encircle a large area that would be secure and could be shaded. By now it was the fifth day after the attack, and Searl and all those at Aquila were confident ABSA would make it.

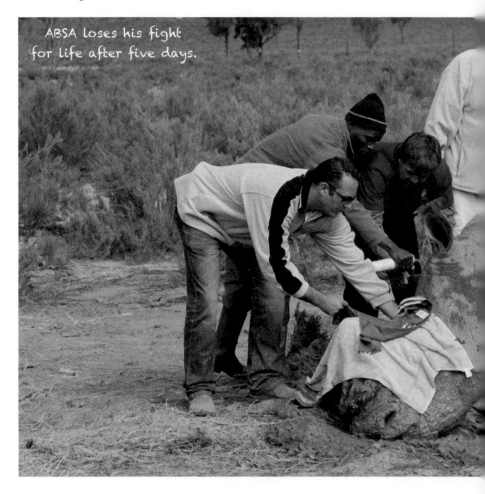

ABSA loses his fight for life after five days.

The carers sat up watching him as usual throughout the night, but when the dawn broke for the sixth time since the attack, the team realised he had died. They had done everything they could to save his life but it hadn't been enough.

The poachers had darted three rhinos and in the end only one had survived. Police trackers and dogs had worked the whole area and

found many signs left by the attackers. It was clear the poachers had watched the reserve for several days from observation posts (OPs), and knew exactly where the rhinos were likely to be at any time of the day or night. When they attacked, they had worked in two teams, one of two people and the other of three. They had darted three of the six rhinos before being disturbed; it is likely their intention had been to poach the horns of all six animals.

The N1 highway is only 2km to the southeast of Aquila. Between the reserve and the highway there is only one farm. The police followed the trail left by the poachers as they fled, and found a jersey and a glove dropped on the ground. They also found where the fence had been cut at their exit point. All the poachers then had to do was cover the few hundred metres of farmland and they could speed off east or west on the highway.

At 2014 prices, the value of the horn from all six Aquila rhinos would have been well over 2 million US dollars (over 20 million rand), so it's easy to see why private reserves were becoming increasingly popular targets. In the Kruger National Park, highly trained rangers, often armed with automatic weapons and sometimes working with Special Forces, were life-threatening opponents. The poachers' expectation would have been that small private reserves would be less well prepared and less lethal.

The news of the Aquila attack spread fast and it became a global story, largely due to ABSA's heroic fight for life.

The poachers had got away with it and, although they left with only three out of a possible 12 horns, it was still a profitable night's work. Pieter de Jager at Fairy Glen and Damien Vergnaud at Inverdoorn both realised the poaching gang would be frustrated yet emboldened by their experience at Aquila. They hastily increased their patrols and security.

Searl Derman still had four rhinos left, so he kept up his security, brought in extra trained men and, once the permits arrived, issued his rangers with weapons. The problems of the Kruger Park hundreds of miles to the northeast were now part of the daily lives of those on the three Western Cape reserves.

Searl Derman is on record for criticising the length of time it took for his weapons licences to be issued. He believes that if his rangers had actually come upon the poachers they wouldn't have been able to defend themselves and would have been shot. He is also on record as being critical of the police investigation that followed the raid: Derman claims it was months before the police interviewed him, which was very frustrating because he had several ideas regarding possible suspects. While waiting for police action he conducted his own investigations, handing over names and information to the police. Searl has also facilitated arrests linked to poaching of shark fins, ivory and other rhino horns. Despite these successes and his efforts to track down the perpetrators of the attack on Aquila, no-one has yet been arrested and his frustration remains.

According to Searl, the police defended their lack of action by explaining that they were working to try and break poaching rings operating on a *national* level; that his case forms part of a body of evidence being collected, and that if the police moved too early they might blow their chances of convicting the major criminal gangs. Time will be the judge!

The poachers drop a jersey as they flee.

Menace stalks the land ....

3

The poacher's moon

The men cast clear shadows on the ground as they crept through the bush. Glinting dully in the full moon were the rifle and the pangas (large African knives, similar to machetes) they carried. A twig snapped and the leader's head whipped round as he silently cursed his noisy accomplice. The moonlight was so bright, the three poachers felt very exposed, particularly as they were in plain view of the Fairy Glen lodge only 500m away ...

Higgins slept as Lady snuffled in the dust a little to his left. She heard the men and turned to face the direction of their approach. The moon cast a perfect shadow of Lady's horned profile on the sand, and she snorted and stamped nervously. Her fear transmitted itself to Higgins who woke and got to his feet, ready to defend himself and his mate. But the rhinos had no chance: the rifle spat out its first dart, which embedded itself in Higgins' shoulder. M99 is the anaesthetic drug used by vets to put animals to sleep when they need to administer treatment or move them; it is also widely used by poachers. A second dart followed, again finding its target and pumping its deadly contents into the rhino. Higgins' instincts were confused – charge his attackers or run? He ran, expecting Lady to follow.

The gunman was quick; as Higgins fled, he reloaded and hit Lady first with one dart then a second. Lady made the other decision and started to charge, then changed her mind and turned to follow Higgins. Her legs had stopped working properly and she collapsed, having staggered only a few steps. Higgins was 90m away when the drug overcame his massive bulk and his nervous system gave up. Forward momentum propelled him into a ditch. The moon's silver silence was broken only by the laboured breathing of the two stricken rhinos.

The men stood absolutely still, waiting to see if the shots and the noise made by the rhinos would produce a reaction from the lodge. They waited only a few minutes before deciding to go to work. Two hacked at the base of Lady's horns with their pangas, while the third sprinted to the ditch where Higgins lay. The male rhino had been given a larger-than-normal dose, his heart had slowed and his breathing was shallow as the first cut of the panga bit into his head. Higgins' attacker was near panic; his two friends were together dealing with Lady while he was working alone. His nervousness pushed him to the edge of terror, and he hacked Higgins' horn in a mad frenzy of brutality. He missed the base of the horn, hit live tissue, causing blood to creep from the wound, then spurt high as his next blow deepened the cut.

Cocky and confident now, the team of two had finished with Lady and walked, almost strolled, to join their accomplice with Higgins in the ditch. One had the rifle slung over his shoulder and on the other's back bounced a sack containing Lady's horns. Higgins' head was covered in blood, one horn was gone and blood bubbled where the poacher had hacked so deep he had gone into the animal's sinuses. The leader pushed his man roughly aside and took over work on the remaining horn.

Two hundred metres away the eland woke, sensed danger, panicked and crashed away through the bush. Startled, the men looked up, but it took just three more powerful panga cuts and Higgins' second horn came free.

The poachers gathered their prizes and, no longer bothering with stealth, ran to the fence to leave. The rhinos had been easy targets. A day earlier a bush fire had been deliberately started to the northeast of Fairy Glen. The helicopter pilot who dropped water on the fire had been able to identify the four places where it had been started with petrol. Animals will always move away from fire, and so it was that Higgins and Lady were down at the southwest end of the reserve that night, only 100m from the fence.

A farm track runs along the outside of the fence and the poachers had left their vehicle close to where they knew they could cut the wire to enter and flee. They had attacked just after 3.00 a.m. Less than

A fire broke out at Fairy Glen a day before the attack and is thought to have been deliberately started.

half an hour later they hurried back the few hundred metres to the fence and then to their waiting vehicle. They had left Higgins dying in the ditch and ran past Lady without a glance.

They drove to the west and were most of the way home when the sun rose over Fairy Glen and exposed their grisly night's work.

To the northeast of Fairy Glen is Inverdoorn, another private game reserve. Inverdoorn's owner, Damien Vergnaud, hadn't slept well. Ever since the attack on Aquila and the killing of their animals Damien had worried about his rhinos. Several times during the night he had got out of bed and gone to the window to look at the moonlit landscape. As dawn broke and Higgins and Lady fought for their lives, Damien shuddered without knowing why. In a few hours his phone would ring, his life would change forever, and he wouldn't sleep for many nights.

Pieter de Jager will never forget Sunday 11 December 2011. At 7:10 a.m. his cellphone rang and Jan, the reserve manager, poured out a torrent of words that seemed to make no sense: Lady, attacked, poached, dying, blood, Higgins, disappeared ... at first the words were all jumbled up, but then they came together, bringing their clear and terrible message. Jan had been driving in the reserve, giving ranger Willem de Wee a lift to work. Willem had looked to his left and seen Lady on her side with her legs in the air.

Pieter was in his vehicle within minutes and driving the 9km from his home to Fairy Glen. As he drove he called the police, his vet, and his friend Johan Botma. He asked Johan, better known as Bottie, to meet him at Fairy Glen as soon as he could. His son, young Pieter, had turned 10 the previous day and the family had held a party at the reserve. He was driving, in a vehicle still filled with yesterday's birthday balloons, towards a nightmare. It seemed insane and surreal.

His feelings of nausea and fear wouldn't help the situation, so he tried to put his own distress to one side as he drove, and wondered why time always seems to pass slowly when you are in a hurry. If the gate to the reserve had been closed Pieter would probably have crashed through it; he didn't even notice it was open as he raced past the entrance.

Pieter ran towards Lady, fearful of what he would find. Chantelle, a Fairy Glen ranger, was on her knees next to Lady, crying and begging her, 'Don't die'. Those words meant she was still alive and, as Pieter realised this, his whole approach changed. Fear, horror, nausea and despair were replaced by an ice-cold anger and a steely determination that Lady would not die. If he let her die, the poachers would have won. He would not allow that. He saw that her breathing was irregular and weak, and both of her horns had been gouged out with cuts that had gone into her sinus passages. Chantelle continually wiped out Lady's nose to help her breathing.

'Where's the bull, where is Higgins?' The voice belonged to Bottie, and hearing it added to Pieter's growing determination and confidence. Lady lay still but her eyes were open and Bottie quickly instructed that they be covered to protect against sun damage. Many people have a particular good friend they would want by their side in a crisis. For Pieter it is his school friend Bottie, who now strode towards where Lady lay, calmly issuing advice and instructions.

The area of flat ground below the lodge had become a hive of activity. Wet towels arrived and were placed over Lady's eyes, and two rangers ran around working a search pattern, looking for Higgins. It was Sunday so Pieter hadn't been able to speak to his vet; he had been able to do no more than leave a message. Pieter and Bottie realised they would have to deal with this themselves and act quickly if they were going to save Lady's life. The wound needed cleaning and sealing, an antidote had to be administered, and antibiotics and dressings were needed fast. The minutes ticked away as Pieter and Bottie worked their cellphones, searching for what they needed to save their rhino.

'I'll go to the local hospital. We'll have to try human antidote, it's our only chance', Bottie was yelling over his shoulder to Pieter as he ran to his vehicle. The local hospital is several kilometres away and Bottie went at it like a Formula 1 driver. Johan Botma stands over 1.8m tall, has long hair tied back in a ponytail and weighs over 135kg. He is a large, kind man with a huge heart. That morning as he burst into Worcester hospital he didn't look at all kind, and nothing was going to stop him from getting the drugs that might give Lady a chance. The hospital staff were immediately sympathetic and helpful, and minutes later he was leaving the hospital again with its entire supply of Narcan, the human antidote, in a box tucked under his arm.

Bottie's absence seemed like an eternity for Pieter, although in fact he was back in just over half an hour. Pieter prayed as he injected the antidote into the soft skin and the vein behind Lady's ear. They were worried that if she lay in this unnatural position much longer her organs might suffer damage. An ear twitched, then both ears moved and her breathing started sounding stronger and becoming more regular.

'Over here, over here, he is here, Higgins is here.' Pieter and Bottie would never describe themselves as athletes but they covered the 100m to the frantically waving ranger in seconds. The male rhino was in a ditch, which was why they had not seen him before. Bad though Lady's wounds were, they were not as bad as Higgins'.

The frenzied hacking had gone deeper into his sinuses and blood frothed and bubbled as he struggled to breathe. The sun's rays were already damaging Higgins' open and unprotected eyes. Rhinos don't have good eyesight and, as Bottie gently placed a wet towel over Higgins' eyes, he wondered if he might not already be too late and Higgins would be blind – if he survived.

Pieter didn't hear the vehicle approach, but Dr Belstead, his vet, who had by now been alerted to the attack, had arrived and immediately took over tending to Higgins. 'We'll need Stockholm Tar,

Ranger Chantelle begs Lady not to die.

Pieter de Jager

Constant hands-on care by all at Fairy Glen seems to have saved the rhinos in their hour of need.

Game ranger Riaan removes two darts from Lady.

lots of it, to seal the wounds.' It was Sunday so the local agricultural store was closed and going to Cape Town would take too long. Fate or God started to take a hand and, just as Pieter began to despair, another vet called saying he had enough Stockholm Tar for both rhinos. Bottie and the vet worked hard and within a few minutes Higgins had been injected with the antidote, painkillers, antibiotics and vitamins. As with Lady, the ears moved first, then he struggled to lift his mutilated head. Pieter, Bottie and their vet watched as their brave patient regained full consciousness.

The sun was high by 11.00 a.m. and the scene was something of a circus as rangers, CapeNature investigators and the police forensic team went about their work. The media were starting to arrive in numbers and the melée was joined by the specialised crime unit, the Hawks. For Pieter, Bottie and the Fairy Glen rangers, the investigation was of secondary importance; what mattered to them was saving their rhinos, and that battle had only just begun.

The full horror of rhino-horn poaching

Bottie
watches
over
Higgins in
the ditch.

Higgins is
a pathetic
sight.

Dr Bellstead
treats
Higgins'
mutilated
face.

Higgins' eyes are protected from the sun with a wet towel.

Bottie points to where Lady was lying ...

... and stands at the fence where the poachers made their escape.

Higgins – a victim of the
poachers' greed and brutality

The aftermath:
Lady faces an
uncertain future.

4

Fight for survival

In the middle of the morning Lady struggled to her feet. As she rose, Pieter and Riaan, a game ranger, noticed the darts hanging from her left side. Riaan put on gloves, removed the darts and handed them to the captain of the investigating Hawks team.

The whole area had been cordoned off and, as the day wore on, Pieter became more and more disappointed with the actions and attitudes of the investigating officials. A constable had been appointed as the lead investigator and she seemed to know nothing about this type of crime. Pieter questioned the appointment and let it be known that he didn't think the Hawks were treating the case very seriously or giving it the right level of priority. However, by evening he decided to put aside his concern over the police's lack of interest and concentrate solely on Higgins and Lady.

Higgins was a pitiful sight and, as Pieter sat by the ditch talking to him, he fought back tears. He didn't know if Higgins could hear him properly or would be comforted by his voice but he needed to feel he was doing something.

'You haven't eaten anything all day.' Bottie sank to his haunches beside his friend and handed him a flask of coffee and sandwiches.

'You know, Pieter, it was a full moon last night.' 'I know,' Pieter replied. 'They call it the poacher's moon.' They sat till late, talking to Higgins and trying to put together the pieces of the puzzle that would help them understand how the attacks had been carried out. Bottie was exhausted and, just after midnight, gave up trying to stay awake and went home to sleep. He would be needed just as much tomorrow and would be useless if he didn't get some rest. Pieter spent the night with his back against a Black Wattle tree, whispering to Higgins. From time to time the rhino's ears moved as if in acknowledgement. Pieter told him he had to fight, that he couldn't leave Lady alone, and that he, Bottie, Denis the ranger, and everyone at Fairy Glen would fight with him. Before drifting into an

Lady leans against a tree as she tries to stay on her feet,

uncomfortable sleep Pieter is convinced he heard Higgins cry; it was an almost human noise, and his own cheeks became wet with tears as tiredness overtook him.

The sun rose on the second day after the attack and Pieter woke, swapping his sleeping nightmare for a waking one. Higgins had moved a little during the night, which was a good sign and meant he was alive. He looked weird and disfigured. Where only two days ago there had been horns, now there was a flat snout covered in Stockholm Tar with cotton wool poking out around the edges.

but the tree gives way and she subsides with it.

Pieter eased his aching joints into action and got up to go and check on Lady. Like Higgins, she was a strange and sad sight. He needed a wash, coffee and something to eat so he trudged wearily up to the lodge.

At the Inverdoorn Game Reserve, Damien Vergnaud hadn't slept all night. The previous morning he had heard the dreadful news – that Fairy Glen's rhinos had been attacked by poachers and were fighting for their lives. First Aquila, now Fairy Glen: the curse of rhino poaching was creeping closer and Damien knew his farm could be next. Inverdoorn is a larger reserve than Fairy Glen and Aquila and its rhinos are free-roaming. Damien knew only too well what dead rhinos with their horns removed look like, and the vision haunted him. How could he protect his animals? There were various options and he started considering them all.

Bottie and Denis were with Higgins and Lady by the time Pieter got back from the lodge. Neither rhino had eaten or drunk since the previous day's attack and Lady was too weak to stand for long. Blowflies and botflies were serious dangers, and all day long Bottie and the reserve staff fought to keep them off by spraying the wounds with a fly-deterrent.

The assault on the rhinos had grabbed the attention of the media, and newspapers, television and radio stations from all over the world had picked up the story. Pieter wanted the right message to get out so he handled all the media himself. Between calls from journalists and reporters he was contacted by Archbishop Desmond Tutu, by a distressed elderly lady in Worcester, and he had many other sympathy calls, both from friends and from complete strangers. While

Top and above: In the end Higgins is able to walk out of the ditch unaided and doesn't need to be lifted by the equipment that has been assembled. These are his first steps towards what will be a long struggle for survival.

condemning the criminals, Pieter assured the media and well-wishers that he would fight all the way to ensure Higgins and Lady survived.

Pieter decided to sit up with the rhinos for the second night. He'd had so much support from people he didn't even know, he now felt as though he were fighting on their behalf too. Bottie had brought a camp bed, some coffee and a lantern and then headed home.

The day before the attack there had been fires to the northeast of the reserve and the helicopter fire fighters had been sure they were the result of arson. Lying on his camp bed above Higgins in the ditch, Pieter stared at the stars and tried to come to terms with events. This had been no random amateur attack; it had been carefully planned, and carried out by professionals. The fire had been lit to test his defences, show the watchers how many staff he had, and move the animals to the southwest fence where they would be easy to attack.

Rhino horn is big business and poachers are not concerned whether the animals live or die. By chance alone, Higgins and Lady were both still alive: and it was this chance reprieve that Pieter clung to during his second night of troubled sleep.

Mid-December is high summer at Fairy Glen and daytime temperatures were getting close to 40 degrees. Lady and Higgins had still not eaten or drunk since the attack. Regular efforts to tempt them with water in buckets had met with no success. They were dehydrating fast and getting weaker by the hour. Bottie built little pools by their heads, to no effect, and wondered whether, despite everyone's efforts, they might lose one or both of the animals.

Not everyone believes in miracles – but Pieter does. As he fretted about the rhinos' growing dehydration, a shadow was creeping over the ground towards him. He looked around and the reserve behind him was no longer bathed in sunlight. Clouds were moving across the sky and the air cooled noticeably. Cool became cold, almost wintry, and then the first raindrops fell. This weather was unheard of in summer and Pieter raised his eyes to the heavens and said 'Thank you'. Somehow, Higgins and Lady had picked up the signal: it wasn't their day to die, and Higgins stretched painfully forwards and drank from a little puddle that had formed next to his head. Pieter believes God sent him a miracle. Within an hour, both rhinos were on their feet and drinking from puddles. Pieter, Bottie and Denis exchanged grins that split their faces. Before, there had been hope and determination, but now they were sure that Higgins and Lady would survive!

Apart from brief visits to the lodge, Pieter hadn't left his animals for nearly three days. But after sleep, food, a shower and a shave it was a new Pieter who arrived back at the reserve just after dawn on the fourth morning. Higgins was standing in the ditch and making noises as if he were calling to Lady. So far, each rhino had fought for its life alone. Rhino eyesight is not good, but Higgins' ditch was deep enough to hide him from Lady anyway. Pieter noticed that Higgins was looking restless, as though he were preparing to climb out of the ditch by himself. They had been discussing ways to help get him out of the ditch. Slings, ropes, a heavy lifting vehicle and other equipment was being assembled for this purpose. But none of this was necessary because, as Pieter watched, Higgins struggled out and stood above the ditch looking confused, as if he didn't know which way to go.

Lady was only 100m away but Higgins went in the opposite direction, unaware how close he was to his mate. The distressed animal crashed through bushes and tripped over his own feet as he blundered off in the wrong direction. Pieter wondered whether the trauma had left him confused, or whether he was disorientated without his horns, or whether the sun's ultraviolet rays had perhaps blinded him. The questions flew through his mind as he watched his friend stumble away, and he had no answers.

Lady moved as well and by Thursday morning, four days after the attack, the previously inseparable pair were 2km apart, at either end of the reserve. The most important thing now was to get them eating again. Bottie had brought bales of hay and they tried with Higgins first. He sniffed it, then tasted it and gently, probably painfully, ate half the bail. Having succeeded with Higgins, Pieter and Bottie had high hopes they would also get Lady eating, but she sniffed the hay and walked away.

Success came the next day when they resorted to bribery and poured molasses over the top of the bale. She couldn't resist the sweet sugary smell and started eating slowly and with difficulty. Pieter was close enough to be able to see a long, deep gash in her upper lip. One of the panga cuts had caught her flesh, and was making eating painful. Nevertheless, after six days of struggle Pieter hoped his problems were easing a little.

For Damien at Inverdoorn the problems were just beginning. The police had now told him they had intelligence that his rhinos would be attacked next. He knew he was in a race against time to take measures to protect his animals. Dehorning was a measure used by many but he did not want to disfigure his rhinos. Large-scale armed security patrols would work, but would be very expensive and he wouldn't be able to keep this up for long. Penning the rhinos so that they could be watched constantly was discounted as they are wild animals and Damien wanted them to be free. He spent long hours on the phone with Alex Lewis, his vet, and together they came up with another strategy. If they could inject the horns with a substance that would dye them permanently and make them impossible to sell, then the poachers would have nothing of value to come and steal. Would this be a workable solution?

Higgins tries to cool off in the dam and
cover himself with comforting mud.

Fairy Glen

**PRIVATE GAME
RESERVE & SAFARI'S
27 (23) 347 8933**

The Fairy Glen investigation

Higgins and Lady were winning their fight
for life and the media storm had passed.
Meanwhile, Pieter de Jager had become
obsessed with the questions of who had
attacked his rhinos and why, where the horns
were now, and whether the police would catch
the poachers. He wanted answers and he wanted
to know what action was being taken.

The initial police presence had looked impressive. A police general, officers of the Hawks specialist crime unit, investigators from CapeNature and a forensic team had all quickly arrived, cordoned off the area and gone about their business. However, when Pieter had given his affidavit to the Hawks captain, he had found it necessary to query why the investigation was being headed by an inexperienced, low-ranking officer. He had been assured the constable would receive help and supervision from experienced senior officers.

Police trackers had worked the ground and discovered the tracks of three men and the place at which they had cut the fence and left the reserve, but there was no sign as to where the poachers had entered Fairy Glen. The reserve isn't difficult to access and one suspicion was that one or all three of the poachers might have masqueraded as clients and gone on a game drive, or even stayed at the lodge.

On Wednesday, four days after the attack, Pieter got a call from a friend who is a vet. This contact, who acted in confidence and on the basis that his identity would not be disclosed, gave Pieter names of suspects, a description of the vehicle they had used, and the location of where the horns might be.

Pieter called the police colonel in Cape Town and was told he was busy with an investigation, but would pass the information to the investigating officer (the constable) who would report progress to Pieter by 7.30 the next morning. Pieter went to bed hoping the police were acting on the information and that he would get news soon.

The next day was taken up with getting Higgins eating again and by evening Pieter remembered he had heard nothing from the police. They already had suspects' names, the description of a vehicle, and even an address – what more did the police need? Pieter began to wish he could take matters into his own hands and do the police work himself. He went home and once again got on the phone to the police. He expressed, in no uncertain terms, his frustration and disappointment, and demanded to know what use had been made of the information he had passed to the police 36 hours earlier. Trails go cold and Pieter knew that it wouldn't be long before this trail was too cold to follow.

His irate phone call produced a reaction and 15 minutes later Officer Fritz from the Hawks rang him. Fritz had an air of efficiency and competence about him and Pieter felt that at last he had an investigating officer who would make progress. They agreed to meet at 9.00 the next morning.

The new investigating officer was 30 minutes early for the meeting, and Pieter started by quizzing him closely about his experience and background. Pieter himself is an ex-police officer, so when Fritz explained his background in the Murder and Robbery unit in Brixton, Pieter was able to evaluate the calibre of the new man.

Now in possession of all of Pieter's information, Fritz left to follow up the potential leads. The address Pieter had been given for the suspects was in Elands Bay on the West Coast. The police went there and the vehicle was discovered in the garage, but the suspects were not there and there was no evidence to link those who had lived in the house to the poaching of Higgins and Lady. It was nearly a week since Pieter had given the information, and a week and a half since the attack, and the trail had gone cold.

Next came a bizarre twist when a relative of one of the suspects – a man known to Pieter – turned up at Pieter's office asking to borrow a small sum of money for petrol. The suspects were small-time game dealers working on the fringes of legality. What was one of them doing coming to ask Pieter to borrow a small sum of money? Pieter's suspicion is that the man was trying to show him that he had no money and therefore wasn't part of the gang. Pieter called the police and the man was arrested at the gates of the lodge. Police enquiries revealed that he was wanted for game-dealing irregularities in Limpopo province and he was transferred there. Pieter is convinced that, had the police investigation moved faster and been more competent, the poachers would have been caught. He had given the police hot information from a reliable source and days had been wasted. Ten days after the poaching incident Higgins and Lady were slowly recovering, and Bottie and Pieter's family persuaded him to go on a planned Christmas break.

Pieter had thought it weird when the man turned up to borrow money but things got even more strange when, on Christmas Day at the family's holiday house, he got a call from a man named Mike who said he worked in exports and wanted to talk about the poaching incident. Mike sounded credible and, when he called Pieter a second time asking him to take a parcel back with him to Worcester (near Fairy Glen), Pieter agreed. The parcel was to be delivered to the holiday house at 7.00 the next morning. Mike had not made it clear whether there was any connection between the parcel and the poaching, and Pieter spent an anxious 10 minutes waiting at the gate for it to arrive.

The parcel carrier turned out to be an elderly woman called Suzy and the parcel was a parrot! It appeared that Pieter was merely being asked to do an innocent favour for his potential informant. As he drove back up from the gates with the parrot in its cage on the seat beside him, he found himself trying to talk to it and wondered whether he was going mad. He discussed the police investigation with the parrot, and asked the bird who Mike was but made no more progress with the parrot than he had with the police!

On the drive back to Fairy Glen, surrounded by his family, he got a 'number withheld' call: 'Careful, you're playing with fire and you'll get burnt'. The threat was clear but was it in relation to anything specific? Was he being warned off following up with Mike? When they got back to Worcester the parrot was collected by a woman who also conveyed a message from Mike, confirming a meeting the next morning at 11.00 and giving Pieter the address.

With officer Fritz next to him, Pieter knocked on Mike's door at the appointed time. Mike is blind and he has two glass eyes, which

The main lodge at Fairy Glen

A plastic refuse rhino

A view across the Fairy Glen reserve

he took out at the beginning of the meeting, saying, 'My eyes have already been removed because I saw too much'. Pieter and Fritz exchanged glances, and Pieter wondered if he had perhaps strayed into a lunatic asylum. However, the fear and tension that Mike transmitted were real and both men felt it. His eyes were not his only injuries – his arms had light scars on them and his wrists bore the telltale marks of having been slashed. Mike's troubles had apparently started when he took a new partner – a Chinese man – into his import/export business in Cape Town. Mike said he began to give information to the police about some of his partner's activities that worried him. Now he spoke of no longer fully trusting the police, and of having 'handled a rhino horn' that had been exported only a week earlier.

The meeting was tense and disjointed, and Mike said he wouldn't talk more fully unless he was guaranteed immunity from prosecution and given police protection. Officer Fritz pointed out that such guarantees were not easy to get and he would need a lot more hard facts. Mike refused to co-operate further without the protections he had asked for, and another trail hit a dead end.

Pieter believes Mike was genuine and had information of real value, but that he was also muddled and badly frightened, and was not prepared to give the police enough information up front to guarantee his protection.

Was the blind man aware of the suspects based on the West Coast? Had they poached the horns to fulfil an order from his Chinese colleagues? The horns weighed approximately 11kg; at that time rhino horn was worth around R495,000 per kilo. Had the poachers been partners in the venture, or were they just hired hands? Their night's work could have earned them R5,000 each, R50,000 each – or much more. Pieter and the police still have many questions, but few answers. At the time of writing – one year and six months after the attack – neither Bottie nor Denis, nor any other staff members at the reserve, had been asked by the police to give a statement. At the time of the attack the rand was worth R9.80 to the US dollar and R14.60 to the pound sterling.

6

Trials and triumphs

Inverdoorn's rhinos – unharmed as yet, and under guard

The attack on the Aquila reserve on 20 August 2011 had sent warning signals to Fairy Glen and Inverdoorn. Both reserves started all-night patrols; but, with limited manpower and rangers spending long days in the field with visitors, intense patrolling could be kept up only for so long.

Inverdoorn had been running patrols with two vehicles and four rangers since the August Aquila attack and, by December, although still fully committed, the rangers were starting to wonder whether perhaps the scourge had passed.

By mid-morning on Sunday 11 December, the news reached Inverdoorn that Fairy Glen's rhinos had been poached, and everyone was back on high alert. Damien Vergnaud was returning to the reserve from Cape Town with a French documentary film crew when he got the news. He and his vet had already discussed and committed to a process that would allow his rhinos to keep their horns – by rendering them valueless. He would now set about implementing the scheme: whatever the costs, he had to keep his rhinos safe.

61

That same night, as the regular patrols combed the reserve, head ranger Wilna Paxton was enjoying a braai (barbecue) with friends on a rare evening off. Just after 10.00 p.m. she realised the zebras were barking frantically and she sensed something was wrong. Wilna wasted no time: she immediately grabbed her rifle, jumped into her vehicle and set off for the 'viewing tower', which is the highest point

Inverdoorn's owner Damien Vergnaud

Head ranger Wilna Paxton

on the reserve. With her lights switched off she made her way up the familiar track to the tower. Much of the reserve was visible from this point and her eyes worked their way slowly round 360 degrees. The animals, and particularly the zebras, were still restless but, other than this worrying sign, Wilna could neither see nor hear anything specifically wrong.

She radioed her patrols who confirmed everything was okay and that they were close to the three rhinos. She reported to Damien at the lodge, then decided to stay on watch for a while, and lit a cigarette as she surveyed the scene.

Her eyes strained into the night and she thought she picked up a faint blue light down on the road along the reserve's boundary. Again she radioed the rangers who said they thought she was seeing a light from a house. Wilna knew there was no house there and her nerves felt jangled as she realised someone with a light was on the road working along their fence. Procedure was that one of the rangers' vehicles conducted mobile patrols, while the other stayed with the rhinos. The patrol that had been with the rhinos then radioed in to say something had spooked the rhinos and they had taken off. The rangers couldn't follow so were now no longer in touch with the three animals.

Wilna again called Damien to report on her concerns, but he had already collected his 9mm H&K automatic pistol and was on his way to join her. She cradled her .22 magnum rifle, and wondered whether she might have to shoot at a human before the night was over. The rifle was fitted with a good light-gathering scope, which she used to look for the rhinos and their possible attackers.

The .22 calibre bullet is a high-velocity round; the military .223 (5.56mm) bullet is only very slightly larger. A .22 magnum bullet with a hollow point will pop a human heart like a balloon, and a shot into the head will almost certainly prove fatal. Shooting an animal to end its suffering was something Wilna handled with regret but no qualms, but what would it be like to have a person in the cross hairs? She would follow the rules and first shout a challenge, then fire an overhead warning shot. If the poachers didn't either run or surrender, and she felt her life or that of her rhinos was threatened, then she would have to make her decision.

She lit another cigarette and was pleased to note that her hands were steady and her palms dry. She had come to terms with her thoughts and knew that if she had to, she would pull the trigger.

Damien arrived and stood next to Wilna. They didn't speak; they didn't have to, each understood what the other was thinking. The radio came to life again as one of the ranger teams reported torchlight inside the reserve. There had been a long flash followed by two shorter ones; clearly the poachers were signalling to one another. Wilna mobilised every vehicle she had and ordered them into the reserve. She instructed that everyone turn on their hazard lights as a crude but effective means of location and identification.

Caution and silence were no longer necessary. It would have been good to catch the poachers, but the main objective was to let them know they had been sighted and, it was hoped, to frighten them off and keep the rhinos safe. Headed by Damien and Wilna, their entire force of rangers was now in the reserve and frantically looking both for the rhinos and the poachers. Damien fired into the air to let the poachers know they faced armed opposition.

If you know what you are doing it doesn't take long to dart a rhino and hack its horns off. Damien and the rangers prayed they wouldn't find their animals dead or dying in pools of blood, with their horns removed.

Another three flashes, this time in a different place. Were the poachers trying to confuse the rangers? Were they testing them or signalling? Headlights were switched on near where Wilna had first seen the lights and a car roared off at high speed. The sound of the vehicle's departure merely heightened the tension. Until the rhinos were found no-one would know whether or not the vehicle had left carrying their horns.

Located near Ceres in the Western Cape, Inverdoorn is the largest of the game farms in the immediate region.

Inverdoorn's baby rhinos take
refuge from the hot Karoo sun.

The police had been called, were on their way to the reserve, and were setting up roadblocks to cut off escape routes the poachers might use. Now the reserve became quiet, and there were no more torch flashes. As the night hours wore on the tension remained high as successive radio contacts kept on reporting that the rhinos had not been found.

By about 2.00 a.m. Damien had decided his rhinos were either dead or they were hiding from the night's activity, and would not be found until the morning. At first light the reserve's guests would be up and expecting to go on game drives, so he had to let some rangers get enough sleep to be able to work properly the next day. Sleep was not an option for Damien and Wilna, however, and together with a pair of rangers, they kept up the search all night.

Dawn is spectacular in the Tankwa Karoo when the sun's first rays creep over the mountains. As the light increased and the patrolling vehicles were wearily heading back to the lodge, Damien spotted a rhino: it was the male, and he was standing up, side on – and both his horns were clearly visible. Thirty metres away the female and her calf slept. All three animals were untouched. The sense of relief was as powerful an emotion as he had ever felt.

It's hard not to suspect that the same gang who nearly killed Higgins and Lady had tried to repeat their poaching at Inverdoorn the next night. It was inevitable the poachers would try again – the value of rhino horn made that a certainty. But the Fairy Glen attack meant that Inverdoorn was on high alert and this, together with the zebras' barking, probably saved their rhinos from sharing the fate of Higgins and Lady.

For several days the confrontation at Inverdoorn continued and the poachers tested the reserve. Damien was under constant pressure to cut off his animals' horns as a way of ending the standoff, but this would mean permanent disfigurement of these African icons. He was determined to find another way. The police warned him to be careful about his own safety, such as not drinking anything he had not personally opened, and he slept with his weapon alongside him.

Damien knew that to keep his rhinos safe, he had to make their horns worthless. However, this in itself was useless unless he could spread the word, so that any potential poachers would know in advance that attacking his rhinos would be a waste of time.

Together with his vet, Alex Lewis, he had decided to inject the rhinos' horns with a triple-action cocktail. The first ingredient was a powerful permanent red dye. Consumers were used to rhino horn presenting as a grey powder; if the powder were bright red it would not look like rhino horn powder – indeed it could be anything – and dealers wouldn't buy it. The second ingredient was an agent that would make the horn or the powdered product fully detectable by X-ray. Of course, many smuggled horns don't go through X-ray machines, but enough do to make this ingredient worth including. The third component of the cocktail was a foul-tasting substance that would leave a long-lasting, very nasty taste in the consumer's mouth.

Damien and Alex were confident that the combined effect of the three ingredients would render the horns worthless. The rhinos would have to be darted and the cocktail injected into their horns. And because the cocktail should spread evenly throughout the entire structure, the dye would need to be inserted by pressurised injection into a number of places up and down the length of the horn.

The rhinos wouldn't be safe until their horns had been treated and *news of the treatment had been widely disseminated,* so while Alex prepared the cocktail and thought about how to carry out the treatment, Damien worked overtime contacting radio, TV and the newspapers to ensure that the message would reach the poachers. While the treatment and media coverage were being arranged, the only way to ensure the animals' safety was physical patrolling, so Wilna and her rangers kept them under observation 24 hours a day.

Throughout this period Inverdoorn was a strange place. The public arrived every day and were taken on game drives as normal,

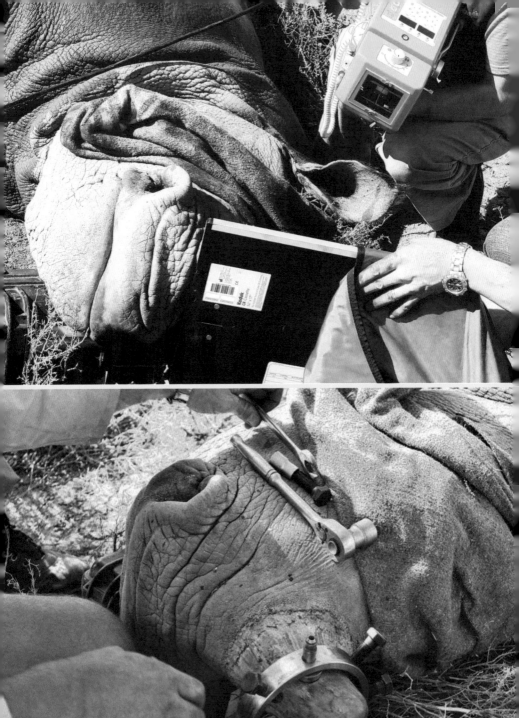

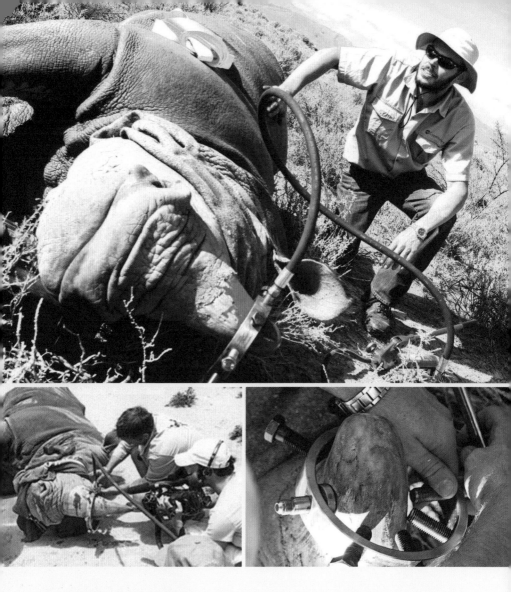

Vets inject red dye into the first of Inverdoorn's rhinos. The triple-ingredient cocktail makes horns detectable by X-ray, is bright red in colour and foul tasting – and it remains active on a semi-permanent basis. Subsequently, many rhinos around the country have been treated in this way in an effort to protect them from poaching.

completely unaware of the frantic activity going on behind the scenes. There was a palpable air of tension and excitement among the reserve staff and, as the days wore on, everyone was high on adrenalin in their determination to keep going. The poachers could return any night, so the team was in a race against time to treat the rhinos.

While the physical security continued, Damien and Alex experimented with techniques to find

Some weeks after treatment the red dye can still be seen on the surface of the horn.

the best way to inject the cocktail under pressure. Alex found some wood with approximately the same density as rhino horn and had several dummy runs to improve the injection technique and ensure effective penetration and diffusion.

By late December they were ready and Damien invited the media, officials from CapeNature and the police to watch the procedure. The plan was to treat all three rhinos in one day, but to treat the female and the calf beforehand so that the technique could be practised before the audience turned up to watch. At 6.00 a.m. on 23 December Damien, Alex, Wilna and a couple of helpers left the lodge in two vehicles and moved into the reserve. The night patrol had been watching the animals and left as Damien's party arrived. It was soon evident that the days of practising, experimenting and rehearsing had paid off. The animals were darted, went down, and both were successfully treated before being given the antidote. This was a procedure that had only rarely been carried out before, and Damien's team had mastered it.

The media and other guests arrived and by 11.30 were watching the male rhino being treated, and witnessed the team working with confidence and practised efficiency. There was another observer too: soon after the male had been darted a white helicopter arrived and hovered overhead for 2–3 minutes before flying off again. It had no identification or registration numbers, and had blacked-out windows. That it had no markings meant the helicopter was flying illegally and, to this day, its identity and purpose remain mysteries.

What only a few people knew was that if, for any reason, the procedure had not worked on the first two rhinos, Damien and Alex had a plan B: Alex would simply have cut their horns off before giving them the antidote, and then done the same afterwards with the male. But plan A had worked to perfection.

There were celebrations that night at the lodge, and everyone shared a real hope that perhaps they had developed an effective new weapon in the war against poachers.

Night falls fast in the Karoo and twilight is fleeting. The reporters and TV crews had left and were broadcasting the story, and Damien and Alex hoped their actions would prove to be enough to save their rhinos – only time would tell. Meanwhile, the patrols had to go on until Damien was confident the story was out there, so that even the dumbest potential poacher knew the Inverdoorn rhino horns were valueless. (In fact, the 24-hour surveillance was to become a permanent part of life on Inverdoorn, and continues to this day.)

In the immediate aftermath of the rhinos' being injected came some bizarre twists. Damien received more than one anonymous death threat. He also received information from the police that he and the rhinos were still targets – the poachers could return to make an example of them, to send a message to other reserve owners that even if they treated their rhinos, they would not be safe.

Damien's father is a French explorer and his mother is Spanish. He grew up in the largely unexplored jungles and bush of central East Africa, and reacted to the threats to his life and his rhinos with a Gallic shrug and a 'what will be, will be' philosophy. He had done all he could and would now call the poachers' bluff, and wait. On the advice of the police he sent his wife and children away from Inverdoorn, but he stayed on with his rangers and his rhinos.

The weeks went by and turned into months; there were no further attacks in the immediate area and the threats stopped. As time passed Damien, Wilna and the rangers relaxed the intensity of their security but kept the rhinos under watch every night through the hours of darkness.

The struggle to stop poaching altogether is far from over and it amounts to a real war – this time the war involves a dispute not over land or political sway, but the last surviving members of an ancient animal dynasty. History may show that Damien and his team not only took part in the war, but that they may have won a very significant battle by developing their horn-treatment cocktail.

In March 2013 we visited Damien Vergnaud and head ranger Wilna Paxton at Inverdoorn. After lunch Damien said he had something he wanted to show us: a new boma had been constructed in part of the lodge area and in it, sleeping under a shelter, were two baby rhinos. Rhinos prove that it is possible to be ugly and beautiful at the same time: these babies displayed the irresistible attraction (the puppy factor) that all young animals possess.

They had arrived at Inverdoorn two and a half months earlier as a pair of traumatised, frightened little orphans. Bundu, the male, was eight months old, and his female friend, Lavinia, was two months younger. Their parents had been killed by poachers when a breeder near Limpopo was attacked and 20 animals slaughtered. They had been put together for company while a new home was sought; and they were lucky because Inverdoorn took them both, so they could continue to find comfort in each other's company.

Their re-homing had been arranged by Inverdoorn vet, Alex Louis, who also supervised their diet. They were fed a mix of milk concentrate and brown rice, and they were thriving. The peace and security of their young lives had been shattered by the poachers so they were very wary of humans when they arrived. Regaining the trust of the two young rhinos presented challenges, but the team worked hard and by the time I met them they were a pair of hugely lovable, trusting, yet rather naughty youngsters.

Lavinia was particularly affectionate and, while I was taking photos of her, she very kindly brought me a slobbered on, chewed lump of wood and thrust it at me through the bars of the boma. I took it, but soon realised it was only on temporary loan because lots of snuffling, snorting and rubbing of the fence followed, so I returned it to her and she walked away with it, unimpressed by the misunderstanding. She was back a few minutes later, but this time without the lump of wood, which she had dropped in the shelter with Bundu for safekeeping.

Months later when vet Jana Pretorius told me that rhinos have a very special sense of humour I thought of Lavinia and her lump of wood, and understood what she meant. Once they had settled, Bundu and Lavinia didn't take long to test their strength and make their first bid for freedom. They just pushed their way out of the boma and went for a walk. They didn't go far and were easily found; and in the months that followed they 'escaped' on several more occasions.

For the time being, at least, Bundu and Lavinia are safe and content. They are watched constantly, their horns have been treated, and they are happy in their new life. I hope they never meet poachers again.

Damien Vergnaud and Bundu

Lavinia and her lump of wood

A fire breaks out at Fairy Glen after the attack.

Higgins trips over his feet and stumbles as he moves away from the action at the dam.

7

Reunited and recovering

A week after the attack Higgins and Lady were both still in an awful mess and had not yet reconnected with one another in the reserve. They looked strange without horns and the huge wounds on their faces were an ongoing reminder of the pain they were in. Flies were both a constant irritant and a danger, and one of the main tasks each day was to spray the wounds with a fly-deterrent.

Both animals had resumed eating and drinking, but they were driven in this respect by their instinct to survive; there was no pleasure in their grazing and their eyes spoke of pain, suffering, and confusion. Lady's eyesight didn't seem to have been affected too much by exposure to the sun's rays, probably because she had been found first and her vacant, drugged, open eyes had quickly been covered with a wet towel. Higgins was found much later and the sun had rendered him almost blind. He seemed lost and appeared to have no sense of direction as he plodded wearily round the reserve, a long way from Lady. Pieter knew that the rhinos' chances of recovery, and the speed of that recovery, would be greatly helped if he could get them back together. However, they were separated by nearly two kilometres, and both were preoccupied with their suffering.

Pieter now developed health problems of his own when he contracted chickenpox. Children often brush this illness off lightly but in adults it can be serious, and Pieter's doctor told him to go to bed for two weeks and avoid exposure to sunlight. Three days later came another emergency call from Fairy Glen – the reserve was on fire. Jan, the reserve manager, told Pieter that helicopters were on the way to help put out the flames and advised him that everything possible was being done to rescue the situation. Bottie had taken over caring for Higgins and Lady on a daily basis so they were in good hands. However, as Pieter lay in his darkened room he thought

Hope for cruelly hacked Fairy Glen rhino

Staff Writer

THE critically injured male rhino at Fairy Glen reserve near Worcester, has made it into the new

After the attack staff painted the wound with a tar mixture to try to prevent it from becoming infected.

"The wound is also dry now. The poachers made two holes in his nose bone, but the skin has grown over one of the holes. They slashed right through the bone into his airway. But he is eating, he is walking around, he sits in the mud, so things are going well with him now."

The female rhino on the reserve was also attacked and dehorned by the poachers, but she recovered more quickly than the male.

At Inverdoorn game reserve near

CALLS FOR INJURED ANIMALS TO BE PUT TO DOWN

Rhinos hanging on after brutal attack

STRUGGLE: The male rhino from Fairy Glen reserve in Worcester is eating and drinking, but is still in a bad way. A photographer has called for the animal to be put down. Picture: CHERYL-SAMANTHA OWEN

Melanie Gosling
Environment Writer

'The female is looking better. I am very positive about her'

THE two Fairy Glen rhino, whose horns were hacked off by poachers after the animals had been drugged, are still alive after eight days – and game reserve owner Pieter de Jager believes they may pull through.

"The female is looking better. I'm very positive about her. The male is still in danger. He's blind, and I'm hoping it's an infection, but the vet said it would be permanent. He walked alright for two days and then walked in circles.

"But yesterday (Sunday) he stood up and walked straight to the water hole and lay in the water for half the day to cool off.

"Then he stood up and I gave him his licence. He ate that and went back to the water," De Jager said.

He had been told that this

was the longest rhino have survived after suffering this sort of injury and after being drugged.

"The vets say that others have died after two days.

"I'm in touch with the vet in Thabazimbi who translocated the rhino here, and a local vet.

A local freelance photographer, Cheryl-Samantha Owen, who visited Fairy Glen near Worcester with De Jager on Saturday, believes the animals should be put down.

She described the rhino as "two highly stressed animals and what felt like a circus going on around them".

"We were allowed to go very close and he (De Jager) went

right up to the animal which should have been left in peace.

"The rhino was obviously very uncomfortable and attempted to go for him," said Owen, who was photographing the animals for National Geographic.

De Jager then took her and two other photographers to the female rhino where they all followed it into the bush.

Owen said later a vehicle full of tourists had pulled up next to the female rhino.

"The next thing they were all following her into the bush. She got spooked and they turned running full pelt to the vehicle

"If he (De Jager) were really concerned he should not be taking tourists to see her," Owen said.

De Jager was taken aback when asked to comment on Owen's claims.

He said she had not mentioned any of this to him and he had got an e-mail from her yesterday thanking him for his assistance.

"That's strange. She asked me specifically to go closer for her photograph.

"When I turned my back she went up even closer to the rhino than I did," De Jager said.

He claimed no tourists were

allowed to get down from the ex-army "buffalo" – armoured vehicles used for game drives.

"The people she saw maybe was my manager, two rangers and another guy from my staff, and myself.

"We were spraying him for flies from 2m and she did come forward and the people did scatter."

Asked for his opinion, Kruger Park vet Johan Malan said it was very difficult to evaluate an animal he had not seen.

"But if it is eating and not losing weight, and is drinking and walking, then it sounds positive," Malan said.

The animal became blind after the attack. It is not clear if it will be permanent. Reserve owner Pieter de Jager believes the rhino will regain its sight.

Lewis to inject a combination of bright red dye and poison into the horns of the three rhino on his reserve. He hopes this will deter poachers. Most rhino horn is smuggled to of the near-blind Higgins smelling fire and not knowing which way to run. He also thought of the other animals being forced by the fire into the fences. He thought of the panic, the noise, the smoke and his animals. Tormented by his thoughts, he abruptly rose from his bed, dressed, got into his vehicle and headed for the reserve.

Four helicopters were circling Fairy Glen as Pieter hurtled through the gates, heading for his second emergency in a month. He saw that the animals were widely scattered as they tried to distance themselves from the flames and the smoke.

Bottie ran up to him as he pulled up at the lodge. 'You're crazy Pieter, the doctor told you to stay in bed. There are lots of us here, we can handle this.' There is no-one in the world that Pieter trusts more but he had to know the answer to his overriding concern: 'Where are Higgins and Lady? We must find them'.

Bottie knew that would be Pieter's first question. 'Lady is safe, and I've got the choppers looking out for Higgins.' He had hardly finished speaking when his radio crackled into life and one of the helicopters reported that Higgins was near the dam. It was a relief to know where he was but it wasn't good news. Higgins was virtually blind and would be highly stressed so he could easily run into the water and drown. The whole scene was chaos, with vehicles going in all directions, helicopters scooping water from the dam, and all the while the smoke and flames getting nearer. A calm animal with full eyesight would have been at great risk, but Higgins was sightless and traumatised.

They drove close to where the rhino stood. He was shaking his head and turning round in confusion. He ran a little way, tripped over his feet and stumbled. Pieter could see his wounds had re-opened and blood was dripping from his face. Suddenly, the confused and terrified Higgins was no longer alone; Pieter hadn't noticed Bottie get out of the vehicle and that he was now walking straight up to Higgins, talking to him as he approached. As he watched Bottie, Pieter thinks he probably stopped breathing – this was very dangerous.

Bottie got to about two metres from the rhino and stood there talking, then he turned his back and, still talking, walked away. Like a tame animal, Higgins followed and Bottie led him to safety. The risk had looked insane but, as Bottie explained later, he was fairly confident he could pull it off – and anyway, on the spur of the moment, he couldn't think of anything else to do. 'By then Higgins knew me, and I think had started to trust me. I had fed him, watered him, sprayed his wounds, and always talked to him whenever I was close. At that time he couldn't see much at all so his sense of hearing and familiar sounds were his main guide. He knew my voice meant food, water, kindness and treatment. He followed me – I don't think there was anything else he could do.' Bottie paused and grinned; 'Except charge me maybe!'

It was a long, hard day but by mid-afternoon the reserve's main buildings were safe, as were the animals, so Pieter went back to bed.

Higgins and Lady had been a pair before the poaching, and Pieter, Bottie and Denis realised it was now vital that Higgins should know Lady was still alive; everyone was sure they would aid each other's recovery. The fire and his lack of vision had combined to make Higgins' recovery much slower than Lady's. He kept walking into trees and bushes, and this repeatedly opened his wounds. He was a sad and pathetic sight and it wouldn't have surprised anyone if he had decided simply to lie down and die. But, along with the urge to reproduce, the survival instinct is powerful in animals and he was not going to give up.

There had been many failed attempts to reunite the two rhinos. Pieter, Bottie and Denis had collected Lady's dung and taken it to Higgins, along with lucerne or hay she had been lying on, or any other material that might have held her scent. Once, they had managed to lead him down off the high ground to the road, to within

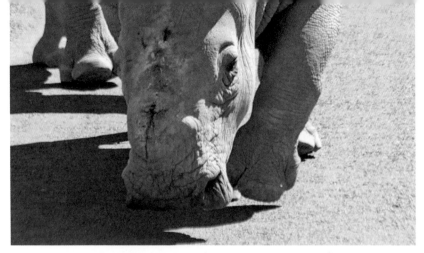

They are still rhinos, but strangely disfigured now without their characteristic horns.

300 metres of Lady, who at that stage was near the dam. He couldn't see her – and she hadn't seen him; he wouldn't cross the road and had turned back up the hill.

Almost a month to the day after the poachers' moonlight attack, Pieter and Bottie tried again to bring the rhinos together. The thinking was that Higgins had followed Bottie during the fire so

Higgins takes a break in the cool sand.

perhaps this tactic could be repeated, allowing Bottie to lead Higgins across the reserve and back to Lady. It was worth a try.

The two men sat in their vehicle and watched the wounded rhino for a few minutes, then Bottie got out, went to the back of the bakkie (pick-up truck) and took a handful of lucerne. Pieter watched as his friend walked slowly towards Higgins, talking as he went. It worked. Higgins followed the voice he had come to trust and even grabbed occasional mouthfuls of lucerne.

Pieter followed them slowly in the truck as the strange pair made their way across the reserve: a nearly 2m-tall human being followed by a hornless rhino acting like a domestic animal. Fairy Glen is relatively small but Higgins and Lady could hardly have been further apart: the distance between them was about two kilometres and it took the odd couple nearly five hours to make their way slowly across the reserve. Bottie hadn't been expecting or prepared for such a long trek and was wearing only shorts, sandals, a T-shirt, and no hat. As the hours ticked by the sun took its toll and Bottie was getting badly sunburnt and his feet were sore and blistered.

Then, suddenly, Higgins stopped. He raised his head and sniffed the air, snorting and making soft mewing sounds. The noises seemed at odds with his bulk, but his body language had changed dramatically and he seemed newly charged with life. He carried on making these noises while casting his head about, allowing his nose to conduct its research.

Bottie backed towards the vehicle and he and Pieter watched and waited. Suddenly, Lady burst from the bushes and ran towards her mate; their heads met gently and they seemed to kiss while the two big men looked on with tears in their eyes.

There is a strong human tendency to interpret animal actions in terms of human behaviour and to attribute human emotions and feelings to animals. Perhaps animal emotions are, in fact, not so different from ours. Certainly in the case of Higgins and Lady, their recovery gathered pace as soon as they were reunited. Lady acted as Higgins' eyes, and the once dominant and sometimes aggressive male now meekly followed his partner.

Immediately after the attack the wounds had been sealed with cotton wool and Stockholm Tar. It didn't take the rhinos long to dislodge this and, after a couple more applications, the 'tar' was abandoned as a wound-sealing treatment.

A patented aerosol for drying out wounds and keeping them clean and free of flies was being used to treat the rhinos' injuries. Apart from initially being startled by the hiss of the aerosol, Higgins was remarkably tolerant of his spray treatments – in fact, he even seemed to enjoy them. Lady, however, reacted quite differently. To quote Denis, 'You had to have your running shoes on because she would

Higgins and
Lady find
one another
at last.

charge you'. They worked out a tactic for spraying her that involved enticing her to the front of the truck while the sprayer was perched on top of the engine. This meant she couldn't easily reach the sprayer and the truck could be rapidly reversed if she charged. As the days, weeks and then months passed, both rhinos regained condition and a measure of confidence.

Despite following Lady closely, Higgins' blindness meant that he often brushed past or into trees, bushes and other objects and opened up his wounds. Nevertheless, the wounds on both animals seemed to be healing. Some 14 months later, the skin had grown back across their faces. The wounds still reopened from time to time and then flies became a danger again but, apart from these accidents, the physical healing process seemed to be going as well as anyone could have expected.

The physical wounds should eventually heal completely, but we will never know about the mental scars. What's more, rhinos' brains must be wired for the presence of horns and there are bound to be repercussions when they are removed. Rhinos use their horns for defence and to push away potential aggressors. Without their horns Higgins and Lady have no defence against other large animals, such as the elephants and buffaloes on the reserve, which have had to be placed in bomas to allow the rhinos to wander freely.

Twelve months after the attack Higgins was seen mating with Lady and everyone at Fairy Glen started hoping this grim story might have a happy ending. The gestation period for rhinos is 15–16 months and their babies are small, so Lady won't show signs of pregnancy until close to delivery.

Rhinos' brains are wired for the presence of horns.

While anaesthetised, rhinos have to be rolled every 20–30 minutes to prevent their body weight from crushing their organs and limbs.

8

Veterinary intervention

Higgins and Lady had survived being attacked by poachers and had made remarkable recoveries. However, although their faces had generally healed, the old wounds kept bursting open; and there was an area next to the stump of Lady's horn that was leaking puss. This final missing piece in the healing jigsaw was a puzzle and an irritant to Pieter.

Higgins and Lady had long since stopped being simply animals on Fairy Glen. They felt more like friends to everyone on the reserve, and not only did Pieter want to do his best for them, he also wanted to atone for the wrong done to them by others. He became convinced that there were still deep-rooted problems with their recovery and that further veterinary help was needed. Medical procedures are very expensive; and Pieter knew that darting both rhinos so that they could be thoroughly examined might be only the start of a lengthy treatment process.

Pieter was considering his financial options when he was contacted by vet Jana Pretorius in July 2013. Dr Pretorius wanted to check on the rhinos' progress and film them for a documentary. Like Pieter, she was unhappy and worried that, 19 months after the attack, Higgins' and Lady's faces had still not healed completely, which indicated deep-seated infection and maybe the presence of maggots.

Higgins ponders his next move as he sizes up the vets.

Veterinary intervention was needed and Dr Pretorius spoke to The South African Veterinary Association (SAVA), which has a rhino fund. The fund is often used for survivors, and to support reserves that have fallen victim to poaching. Pieter's prayers were answered when Dr Pretorius called him asking for permission to come and treat his animals, and use the treatment as part of a workshop for vets who needed to know more about working with injured rhinos.

The Fairy Glen attack had highlighted the need for vets who don't normally deal with wildlife to gain more experience wherever possible. The attention Higgins and Lady had received immediately following the attack was good emergency treatment, but there had been no-one present with first-hand rhino experience – a handicap that had proved disastrous following the attack on Aquila.

Thursday 17 October 2013 started like any other day for Higgins and Lady, who weren't aware that a small army of people was about to gather at Fairy Glen, and that they – the rhinos – would be the focus of attention. Pieter and his ranger team used lucerne to tempt the rhinos into a boma so that they would be readily available to the vets the next morning. Higgins had other ideas. Nearly three tons of rhino can push its way out of most structures – and that's what Higgins did.

When over 40 vets, photographers, a film crew and others arrived the next morning Higgins and Lady had gone walkabout! Luckily, they hadn't gone far, but when Dr Pretorius darted Lady, the rhino decided to put as much distance between herself and the humans as possible. Perhaps the memory of the last time she had been darted caused her to panic and flee, and she ran right to the back of Fairy Glen where there is a *koppie* and thick bush in which to hide. Vets, rangers, observers and cameramen leapt into their vehicles and a convoy sped off in her direction.

The veterinary team was led by doctors Jana Pretorius, Gerhard Steenkamp and Johan Marais, and they were supported by other veterinary specialists and by experienced helpers. They soon caught up with the by now immobilised Lady, and sprang into action. Dr Pretorius took on the role of organiser and anaesthetist, and Dr Steenkamp and Dr Marais worked together as the surgeons.

The team's goal was to attend to the rhinos' facial wounds, discover why they hadn't fully healed, and take appropriate action. But there was an associated challenge: to ensure that the animals suffered no ill effects from the prolonged period of enforced immobility during the operations. They had to be rolled over every 20–30 minutes to prevent their body weight from crushing their limbs, causing muscle necrosis and eventual kidney failure. Their heartbeat and respiration had to be monitored, as did the effectiveness of the anaesthesia.

Under the small remaining stump of Lady's front horn they discovered deep-seated infection. The decision was taken to remove the stump surgically so that the infection could be properly treated. The infected wound had gone deep, right in as far as the paranasal sinus.

Dr Steenkamp cleaned the wound channel and applied several dressings, employing human dressing materials never used on rhinos before.

Once the wound had been cleaned, and the dressings applied, Lady effectively had a hole in the front of her face. To keep the dressings in place the vets screwed a lid over the hole using special long, hi-tech, stainless steel screws, made by Roth Medical, that went down into the bone. Lady didn't know it, but she was having a rhino face-lift! Her treatment had been pioneering and had involved three veterinary 'firsts' in South Africa: it was the first time vets had used interorbital blocks to ensure that nothing was felt by the patient; Dr Steenkamp had carried out the first surgical removal of a horn (using only a scalpel); and it was the first time hi-tech human dressings had been used on a rhino.

While she was under the anaesthetic, Lady's eyes were examined, X-rays were taken of her head, samples of puss were removed from the wound and, by the time she woke with her new face screwed on, she was a much better understood medical patient.

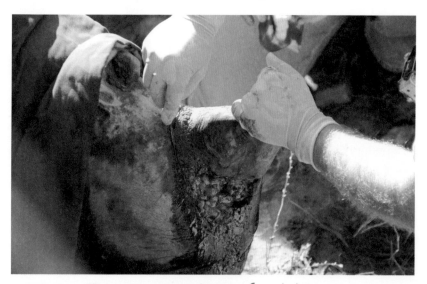

The remaining stump of Lady's horn
is removed with a scalpel.

Higgins' pre-op drama presented differently. After being darted he stayed on his feet for seven or eight minutes while the vets became matadors, using items of clothing to flap at him and get him to move to the shade where they could work comfortably.

Dr Jana Pretorius had explained that rhinos are special animals and that they have a sense of humour. Footage of Higgins shot at this time supports that notion. Minutes after being darted he was still on his feet, watching with a bemused air while Dr Pretorius did her best matador imitation to attract his attention. Higgins refused to react: he neither charged, nor retreated. It was hard not to imagine him giggling and thinking, 'If I just stand here and do nothing, what's she going to do for an encore?'. There was something surreal about the apparently drunk, hornless rhino peering at the improvised matador.

Eventually, on increasingly wobbly legs, he was goaded and pushed into the shade, where he was blindfolded. But he still hadn't quite given up and, in spite of seven pushing and shoving human attendants, he simply sidestepped them and wandered out into the sun again. His handlers had to be careful because he could have collapsed at any time, and puny human bones under two and a half tons of rhino would snap like twigs. Eventually he was manoeuvred back into the shade and could fight the drugs no longer. A relieved team of vets was able to get to work.

There was no stub of horn left in Higgins' face and his infection channel didn't go as deep as Lady's; however, there were other problems. The skin that had healed across his face was of poor quality and Higgins still thought that he had a horn – he often rubbed his face on bushes and trees, regularly reopening the wound just as it was starting to heal. For now, the vets cleaned out his abscess and dressed it and, while he was under anaesthesia, took the opportunity to check his eyes and thoroughly X-ray his head.

In pursuit of lady, who has fled from the medical team

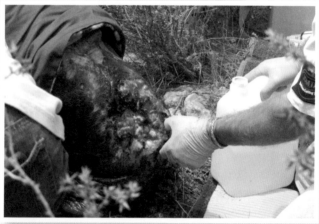

Lady's wound is thoroughly cleaned and disinfected.

Gauze is applied to her wound before a protective plate is fitted to her face.

Lady is about to be woken up following her treatment.

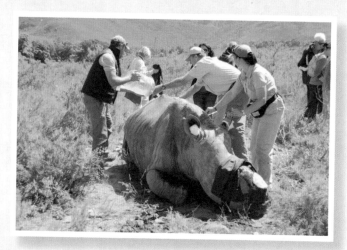

Higgins, although darted with anaesthetic, resists succumbing to its effect.

Pieter de Jager and his son share Higgins' and Lady's stress.

Nearly a month after the procedure in October, Higgins had a fight with a buffalo. On 18 November he was darted again and, like Lady, had a plate screwed onto the front of his face. Lady was also darted and examined and 'punch biopsies' were taken from behind her ear and placed on her face as skin grafts to assist with the regrowth of healthy tissue. The vets hoped that the infections would drain, granular tissue would grow across – under the plates – and that this would be followed by stronger, healthy skin that would cover their faces where their horns had once been.

By now, all those involved knew there would be no quick fixes for Higgins and Lady. Both Pieter and the veterinary team realised that effective treatment and permanent healing of their faces would take months, if not years. It would be an ongoing project: the brutal actions of the poachers, carried out in minutes, had condemned Higgins and Lady to years of uncertainty, stress and suffering. On the positive side, vets Pretorius and Steenkamp and the South African Veterinary Association would remain committed to treating these victims of the brutality of poaching.

On 9 January 2014, two years and 21 days since the poachers' attack, the vets returned to Fairy Glen for the third time. The familiar vehicles drew up and the team assembled. Tempted by bales of lucerne, the rhinos approached. As they did so it became clear that, although the covers carefully screwed onto their faces in late November had stayed in place until fairly recently, they had now both managed to get rid of them. Higgins was known to have discarded his about two weeks earlier, and Lady had finally got rid of hers only the day before. Lady's face still looked an angry mess, but Higgins seemed to be healing well. Because Lady had twice run off before when darted and was expected to do so again this time, Jana Pretorius requested that the vehicles be positioned in such a way that Lady's direction of flight could be closely watched. Both rhinos were grazing on lucerne beside one of the vehicles; Pretorius took careful aim, and there was a muted 'phut' from the gas rifle. The aim was good, the dart struck home and, true to form, Lady wheeled round and demonstrated just how fast these huge beasts can run if they want to. All the vehicles raced off in pursuit and Lady finally stopped about one and a half kilometres away. Higgins wasn't far behind; head down, he followed her scent trail.

As soon as Lady slowed down, the team of well-practised experts jumped from their vehicles and set to work. Lady went down in a good position, which meant that turning her and carrying out all the monitoring tasks was made easier. For the duration of the procedure, Higgins watched from a safe distance.

Vet Jana Pretorius darts Lady for her third treatment.

Steenkamp, backed by the efficient, relaxed team, worked on Lady's face. Loss of the cover had caused some damage to her skin graft. The wound had nevertheless closed up slightly, there was no infection, and there was some healing or granulation tissue – all good signs. Based on experience with other animals' wounds, the vets expected healing to take about a year, and the wound would need to be kept covered and moist. To ensure these conditions the team attached a new cover, and this time would come back sooner – in about three weeks – before Lady started rubbing it again. Lady wasn't aware of what was going on: the anaesthetic meant she was mostly on another planet, and she only raised her head when holes were being drilled for the screws that would secure her face cover.

Just over an hour after she went down Lady was given the antidote and, minutes later, got shakily to her feet. She was now wearing a pink circular cover on the front of her face, this time held in place by more screws – longer ones than previously – and secured by washers. She sauntered off as if nothing had happened, and suddenly Higgins materialised at her side. Perhaps, had he realised he would be next, he would have made himself scarce instead of watching over his mate.

Higgins had shown in many ways that he was a force to contend with. He had escaped from the boma the day before his first big operation in October. Once darted he had refused to succumb to the vets' matador techniques as they tried to corner him; then, after he had been manoeuvred into the shade, he had simply walked out into the sunshine again. A month after the last operation the vets had been called back to fit him with a face plate like Lady's because he had decided he still had a horn, and had picked a fight with a buffalo.

Lady's darting had gone according to pattern, but, if Higgins' earlier behaviour was anything to go by, they could now expect the

Lady succumbs to the vet's anaesthetising dart.

Holes have to be drilled
into the bone for screws.

Lady's protective
cover is fitted.

unexpected. Higgins didn't disappoint. The first dart fell out and he ran off a short distance; Jana took aim again and the second dart stayed in and discharged its contents. Higgins ran around a little, then slowed down and was approached by the vets doing their matador act to attract his attention and lure him to a place suitable for the operation. Always a good sport, Higgins chose instead to continue with the matador game: as the 'bull', he charged Dr Steenkamp three times.

He had been darted near a road and he walked up and down it, across it, and off to either side, following the flapping cloths and refusing to give in to the drug. On the road he adopted a high-stepping gait, probably because he was no longer sure where his feet were. For nearly 10 minutes he put on a great show, and it was impossible for those present not to feel huge affection for this stubborn, brave, and rather comical-looking hornless rhino.

Lady sports face cover number three.

When eventually he did go down it was in a little gully and he was lying in an awkward position. The vets began their work, hoping to roll him into a better position. His face was much better than Lady's and required mainly cleaning and dressing. Fortunately the wound from his fight with the buffalo had healed to some extent and reduced in size. However, because Higgins had once again resisted the anaesthetic, ending up in the 'dog-sitting' position – dangerous for his muscles and ligaments – fuller treatment had to be put on hold until the next session. It was not possible to assess how healthy or how thick the new skin was, and the dressing could not be secured by a screwed-on cover.

He was given the antidote, got to his feet, and stood looking confused and sorry for himself as the team made their way back to their vehicles and drove away.

Always up for a game, Higgins plays the part of the bull.

This was the situation at the time of writing *The Poacher's Moon*. The treatments will continue until they are successful, whether it takes weeks or months. The South African Veterinary Association Rhino Survivors Fund is in place to help the victims of the curse of rhino poaching. Sadly, Higgins and Lady are not alone and, increasingly, the practices and skills being developed by specialist vets like Pretorius and Steenkamp are being called on to treat other survivors.

Rhinos are particularly susceptible to stress, and this is why many poached animals die. Dr Jana Pretorius is adamant that Higgins and Lady are probably only alive today thanks to the actions taken by Pieter de Jager and his team immediately after the attack. 'Pieter doesn't realise it, but I think the only reason these rhinos survived and so many others died is that they sat and spoke to them 24 hours a day. Because the voices were familiar to the animals they were comforted, and their stress levels and loneliness were reduced.'

Higgins leads the vets a merry dance.

Higgins falls in an awkward position.

Higgins' wound requires only cleaning and dressing.

Higgins and Lady have
been subjected to
a series of veterinary
procedures in an effort
to heal their faces.

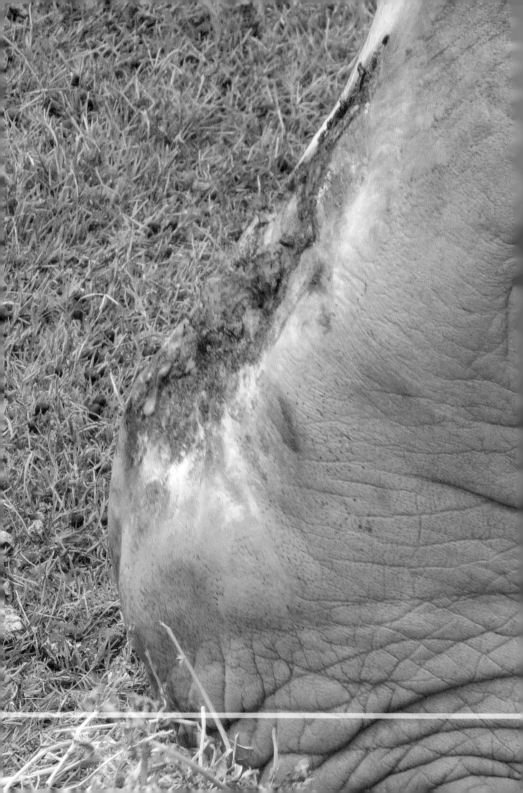

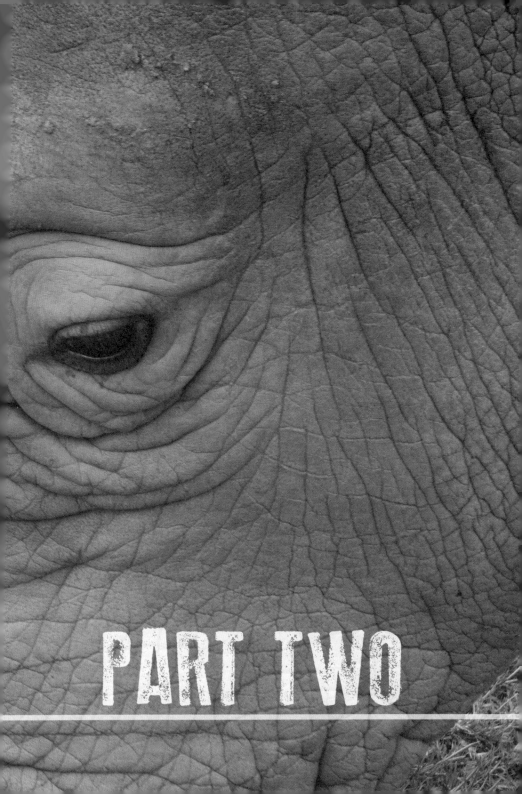

PART TWO

Hook-lipped or black rhinos are targeted as relentlessly as their white rhino cousins.

9

A species under threat

Rhinos – both black and white – have been hard hit by trophy hunters over the years. By the early 1960s, most of the remaining wild white rhinos (fewer than 500), lived in what is now the Hluhluwe-iMfolozi Park in KwaZulu-Natal. The white rhino species was saved from extinction largely through the efforts of South Africans Ian Player, vet Toni Harthoorn and other dedicated conservationists who campaigned during the 1960s to save the species. By the time Higgins was born the population had recovered to about 20,000 animals, but that was as good as it would get.

While white rhino numbers were at their lowest in the 1960s, the black rhino population was healthier, at up to 70,000. But by the end of the 1980s poachers had taken a terrible toll on black rhino numbers too: only about 5,000 remained, as estimated in 2013 by the IUCN African Rhino Specialist Group.

The official figure for the number of white rhinos poached in South Africa in 2000, the year Higgins was born, is seven. As he entered his teens 13 years on, that figure had risen to an alarming and staggering 1,004 in 2013: a white rhino was poached every 8 hours 45 minutes in South Africa during the year – nearly three animals a day!

The table below gives the poaching figures for white rhinos since 2000. At the time of writing (early 2014) the annual birth rate may not be keeping up with the numbers being killed by poachers. A recent census in the Kruger National Park indicated numbers may have fallen from an estimated maximum of 12,000 to a possible low of 8,400. If poaching continues to increase at its present rate, and if the tipping point hasn't already been reached, it certainly soon will be – and then it will be downhill again towards extinction in the wild.

South Africa and Zimbabwe are the main sources of horn, and in recent years poaching in Zimbabwe has returned to levels not seen since the 1980s. At least 123 rhinos were poached in that country in 2008,

POACHING INCIDENTS

White rhinos killed in South Africa

2000 –	7
2001 –	6
2002 –	25
2003 –	22
2004 –	10
2005 –	13
2006 –	24
2007 –	13
2008 –	83
2009 –	122
2010 –	333
2011 –	448
2012 –	668
2013 –	1,004

(The above are official figures released by the Department of Environmental Affairs)

which was the highest number recorded since 1987. The methods used and actions taken by many of the poaching gangs indicate military training, and the AK47 was a favourite weapon for Zimbabwe's poachers.

It is worth noting that South Africa's neighbours, Namibia and Botswana, are both less affected by poaching. Many people say these countries are better policed and have less corruption; and some point to the death penalty in Botswana as evidence of a tougher system with effective deterrents leading to lower crime rates.

In 1993, the People's Republic of China announced a total ban on the sale, purchase, import, export and ownership of rhino horn. Shop owners, dealers and stockists were given six months to dispose of their stock. Perhaps most importantly, rhino horn was removed from the list of state-sanctioned medicines.

The Chinese measures worked and contributed to holding rhino poaching at relatively low levels until 2002, when there was a sudden fourfold increase on the previous year's figures. This coincided with Vietnam becoming the world's main user of rhino horn. By no means all rhino horn that ended up in Vietnam was poached: a significant proportion was acquired legally. Permits to hunt rhinos were issued to trophy hunters who then exported their trophies quite legally, covered by CITES (*Convention on International Trade in Endangered Species of wild fauna and flora*) permits. By 2010, 70% of trophy hunters shooting rhinos in South Africa were Vietnamese.

These 'legal' hunts enabled unscrupulous operators to run rings around the law and made a mockery of CITES 'protection'. The transformation of Vietnam's economy since the end of the war with the United States has been dramatic. As with the other 'Asian tiger' economies, consumer spending power has risen and, as a result, some species of wildlife have suffered and come under ever-increasing pressure. One of the worst affected animals is the rhino.

In 1977 CITES imposed an international trade ban on rhino horn, yet in 1978 South Africa reported the export of 149.5kg of rhino horn to Hong Kong. Further indications of South African government complicity in rhino horn trafficking came in 1982 when Dr Esmond Bradley Martin published his book *Run Rhino Run*. The 149.5kg declared in 1978 was shown to have originated from the former Natal Parks Board. However, records in Hong Kong, Taiwan and Japan show another 860kg as having entered these countries from South Africa at that time.

At $65,000 a kilo, rhino horn is now worth as much as gold or cocaine.

The Natal Parks Board had been a major supplier of rhino horn but stopped selling it after 1978 in order to comply with the CITES ban. By the end of 1979 most South African provincial authorities were officially prohibiting the export of rhino horn. However, Japanese records show that in 1980, three years after the CITES ban, 587kg was imported into Japan from South Africa. The origins of this horn were thought to be Angola, Namibia, Zambia and Tanzania. Whatever the origin, South Africa was part of the routing and these records indicate the regrettable ineffectiveness of international agreements. As with all commodities throughout the history of both legal and illegal commerce, the reality is that *whenever there is a demand there will be a supply*.

PRINCE BERNHARD, THE WWF, AND EX-SAS SOLDIERS

In 1981, in discussion in Nigeria with the WWF's president Prince Bernhard, Dr John Hanks – an internationally respected biologist and conservationist with a doctorate from Cambridge, and head of the WWF's Africa programmes – had raised the issue of the extent of rhino poaching and its catastrophic effect on populations. The prince was dismayed to learn that millions of dollars were being spent on security, while very little was being spent on investigating those involved in the actual trade. Prince Bernhard indicated to Hanks that he would like to finance an exercise to track down and expose the smugglers. The prince stressed that he would fund this himself as he believed it was not appropriate that it be seen as a WWF project, or that the money go through WWF accounts. A noble and sensible approach but possibly also a naive one – the idea had come from the WWF president, and was progressed by its head of Africa programmes, so there was no way this exercise would ever be seen as anything other than something in which the WWF had a hand.

At the end of 1987 Hanks flew to London to meet Sir David Stirling, founder of the SAS (Britain's elite army unit, the Special Air Services). Sir David was running a private security and intelligence company called KAS Enterprises, whose employees were almost exclusively ex-members of the SAS. KAS was eventually contracted to set up operations in southern Africa to investigate and expose the illegal trade in rhino horns. The exercise became known as 'Operation Lock' and ran for a few years under the control of the KAS managing director, Colonel Ian Crooke.

According to ex-South African security branch policeman Mike Richards, between February and July 1990 the Operation Lock team sold 98 rhino horns to smugglers. Throughout its time in operation there were claims that Operation Lock was dealing in ivory and rhino horn. If these claims are true it is likely the explanation would be that it was a necessary part of their intelligence gathering and infiltration operations. Whatever the excuse or explanation, it is astonishing that an outfit that had been put in place by senior figures in the WWF should be dealing in animal products.

In this shadowy world, inhabited by shadowy people comfortable living in the shadows, it is unlikely that full details of KAS operations and all those involved in them will ever emerge. We can be sure, however, that the WWF, and agencies in both the British and South African governments, must have had a good idea of what was going on.

There are those who believe that the end justifies the means and that Operation Lock had some success. It has even been claimed that Operation Lock was partly responsible for the reduction in poaching during the 1990s, although this was probably more the result of the Chinese ban in 1993.

There are basically two types of poacher: the simple, subsistence-level tribesman who is hunting for the pot or killing for someone else, and the sophisticated, highly resourced criminal using helicopters, dart guns and advanced communications equipment. Very often, of course, the former works for the latter.

Since 2003, as the number of rhinos being poached has grown, so has the corresponding number of Vietnamese 'hunters' coming to South Africa to hunt them in order to procure their horns as 'trophies'. South African government records show that in 2003 at least 20 rhino horns were exported to Vietnam (there were nine trophies with both horns, and two single horns). In 2005 the figure was 12 trophies (24 horns); in 2006 the number had increased to 146 horns, in 2008 it went down again to 98, then 136 in 2009, and 131 in 2010.

This permitted hunting allows horns to be kept as trophies and exported by the hunter under the cover of a CITES 'trophy certificate'. In the years between 2005 and 2010 at least 659 horns were taken in this way. Using average horn weights, this means that a staggering 2–3 tons of rhino horn were legally exported to Vietnam. This produces a black market value of between $200 and $300 million, while the trophy fees would have come to just $20 million. This is not just a legal anomaly, it's a loophole through which you could fly a jumbo jet, and the profits are huge.

By 2012 the Vietnamese hunters had started to be replaced by hunters from Eastern Europe, notably from Poland and the Czech Republic. These new 'sportsmen and -women' are being recruited by the Vietnamese horn dealers, who offer paid-for holidays in South Africa in return for names on licence applications and the presence of the licence holders when the animals are shot.

The diplomatic bag has long been used by embassies to move sensitive items in and out of host countries. In strict Moslem states where alcohol is prohibited, the 'dip bag' has enabled diplomats to enjoy a glass of wine with dinner. So it is with rhino horn: the bag provides the opportunity to smuggle with impunity.

In mid-2008 Tommy Tuan was arrested by the police at a hotel in Kimberley. He had just taken delivery of a consignment and in his room they discovered over 20kg of horn, a handgun, ammunition and a large amount of cash. Tuan was using a car with diplomatic number plates and its registered owner was Pham Cong Dung, the political counsellor at the Vietnamese Embassy. Two years prior to this incident

The CITES treaty – controlling, limiting and banning trade in endangered species – is often hailed as being the only effective barrier between many species and their extinction. CITES Appendix 1 and II listings have had their successes in promoting sustainability but, as we have seen with rhinos, the system is open to abuse; and, without the conscientious compliance of member states, its effectiveness will remain limited. As long as the abusers (individuals, organisations and governments) can operate largely unchecked, CITES will remain an expensive good idea.

The CITES treaty originally came into effect in July 1975. South Africa was a founding member, China ratified it in 1981, Thailand in 1983, Vietnam in 1994 and Laos in 2004. This means that all the nations key to the rhino-horn trade are CITES members. The green movement has called CITES 'the animal dealers' charter', and many animal rights activists claim it promotes rather than stops trade!

In 1994 South Africa proposed changing the white rhino CITES listing from Appendix I (threatened with extinction) to Appendix II (trade to be strictly regulated). The conference members allowed this and, as we have seen, 'hunting' operations eventually played a major part in supplying Vietnam's horn market after 2003.

the police had obtained evidence that the embassy's economic attaché, Nguyen Khanh Toan, was using the diplomatic bag to smuggle rhino horns out of South Africa to Vietnam. Dung's Honda was impounded by the police but later returned after Dung had given the explanation that his car had been borrowed by Nguyen Khanh Toan.

In November 2008, TV footage showed an embassy official receiving a number of horns from a known trafficker. The footage was shot outside the embassy and Dung's Honda was parked close by. The person who received the horns was Ms Vu Moc Anh, who was the embassy's first secretary. The ambassador told a newspaper that Ms Vu Moc Anh was helping friends and wasn't involved in horn smuggling. Normally, Dung's Honda would have been parked inside the embassy, and his explanation for its being parked outside was that he wasn't using it that day. Vu Moc Anh was recalled to Hanoi to explain her part in the incident, and Dung left South Africa some while later. Despite the evidence that embassy staff were involved in handling rhino horn, no action was taken by the South African government, seemingly because it wanted to avoid damaging diplomatic relations.

The 'Boere Mafia' was a South African organisation allegedly involved in canned hunting (controlled hunting in a limited area, often using animals that have been bred for the purpose) and poaching. Members of the organisation were accused of various offences, including rhino-horn poaching. However, in October 2010 the case against them was dropped on the grounds that the charges stemmed from arrests made four years earlier, and the prosecution case was based largely on the questionable testimony of a convicted felon. (It is suspected that this witness was a member of the gang and was frightened into not testifying.)

Following a 15-month investigation called 'Project Cruiser' into another suspected poaching scheme, suspect Dawie Groenewald and accomplices found themselves facing 1,872 counts of racketeering, money laundering, fraud, intimidation, illegal hunting and dealing in rhino horns. Dubbed the 'Groenewald Gang', Dawie and his 10 co-accused (which included his wife, other professional hunters, veterinarians, safari operators, and a helicopter pilot) have so far managed to delay the hearing of their case.

Alleged rhino horn syndicate 'mastermind' Dawie
Groenewald on his farm near Musina, South Africa

Rhino organisations, sanctuary employees, conservationists
and members of the public protest against rhino poaching
at Johannesburg Zoo, November 2011.

The gang first appeared in court in September 2011 and there were subsequently a number of postponements. They again appeared in October 2012, and their counsel managed to obtain yet another delay until May 2013. In May it was decided that the case would be heard in the high court in Pretoria in July 2014. Some conservationists fear that the Groenewald Gang prosecution may end up going the same way as the Boere Mafia case, with charges either being dropped or greatly watered down.

The record of the South African authorities bringing successful poaching convictions is poor, and when convictions are obtained the punishment has often scarcely been a deterrent. However, when poachers appeared before presiding magistrate Prince Manyathi in 2010 and 2011, leniency was not shown for Xuan Hoang who was a Vietnamese courier caught at OR Tambo airport (Johannesburg) in March 2010. Manyatti gave him 10 years without the option of a fine. Then in 2011, suspected poachers Doc Manh Chu and Nguyen Phi Hung, who had been arrested at the time of the World Cup, also came before Manyathi. He convicted them and handed down sentences of 12 and eight years, once again with no option of fines. Conservationists, pro-wildlife activists and campaigners applauded the sentences.

Bilateral talks between South Africa and Vietnam took place in September 2011. It was announced that the parties had agreed to work towards an MOU (Memorandum of Understanding), which would include collaboration on wildlife protection, law enforcement and the management of natural resources. The MOU was eventually signed 15 months later on 10 December 2012.

Vietnam may have taken over from China as the world's leading consumer of rhino horn, but Vietnam is by no means the only country involved in this trade. In the 1960s and early 1970s Hong

Kong was a leading player; between 1970 and 1977 Yemen recorded receiving 22.5 tons of horn, which represented 7,800 dead rhinos; and Taiwan was also a significant consumer.

Today Laos, Thailand, Cambodia, Hong Kong and Taiwan may not account for as much rhino horn as Vietnam, but all these countries are traders and/or consumers.

The Far Eastern consumers of wild animal products are not inherently bad people; they are only following beliefs and traditions that have existed for thousands of years. There are now reports that the consumption of shark-fin soup in China is decreasing. For many years campaigners such as WildAid and others have been working to increase public awareness of the realities of eating shark-fin soup. More recently, Chinese superstar basketball player Yao Min joined the campaign to ban the import and sale of shark fins. The cruelty, the unsustainability of supply (which could lead to extinctions) and other factors have been highlighted and, as a result, demand has fallen.

Shark conservation campaigners should not slacken their efforts but should be encouraged by this positive sign and continue to use these clearly effective methods to spread their message. The shark-fin example shows how public awareness and education in the Far East can be more powerful than military weapons and laws when it comes to reducing demand ... and without demand there is no need for supply.

Jo Shaw of the WWF in South Africa commented: '... South Africa's rhinos are up against the wall. These criminal networks are threatening our national security, and damaging our economy by frightening away tourists. Rhino poaching and horn trafficking are not simply environmental issues. They represent threats to the very fabric of our society.' (Cape Times 20/01/14)

Rhinoceros
horn products
packaged
for use as
aphrodisiacs

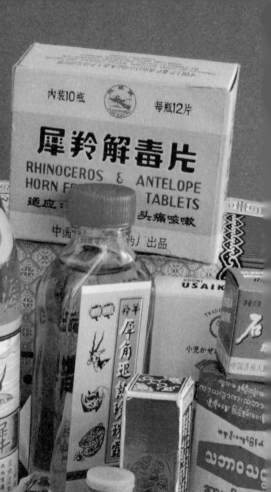

10

Medicine and myth, delicacy and death

What is it that makes rhino horn so valuable that humans are ready to kill - and risk dying - for it? At the heart of the issue is 2,000 years of culture and belief. In Arabia, and particularly in Yemen and Oman, rhino horn was prized as a material for making jambiya and khanjar (types of Arabian dagger) handles. In Vietnam some 9,000 health centres practise traditional medicine and most state hospitals have departments that specialise in it.

For medicinal use the horn is ground down in special dishes and water is added. It's recommended that users drink between 0.5g and 1g daily for general healing and reducing pain. A Vietnamese pharmacopoeia lists rhino horn for treating headaches, fever, delirium and convulsions. Various rhino-horn products are supposed to act as aphrodisiacs, to enhance male performance, reduce temperature and cure arthritis, back pain and many other ailments. Vietnam's affluent young elite are big consumers, using rhino horn to counter hangovers, and they often mix rhino horn with cocaine and other recreational drugs.

For many reasons cancer is a huge killer in Vietnam. According to the World Health Organisation (WHO) up to 200,000 people in Vietnam are diagnosed with cancer each year, and there are

Left: A stall in Myanmar selling animal skins, skulls, horns and other body parts used in traditional medicine

Below: Jars of various animal body parts, such as shark fins and assorted tongues, in a Chinese pharmacy in Japan

75,000–100,000 cancer deaths annually. The country has a population of about 90 million and the government is simply not capable of treating all of its cancer sufferers. Treatment is expensive, hospitals are overcrowded and equipment is often antiquated. Little wonder then that when word goes round that rhino horn is a miracle cancer cure, desperate patients and their families will obtain it if they can. When a senior government official claimed on the internet that rhino horn had cured his cancer, the demand skyrocketed.

There's a common but mistaken belief that rhino horn is made of hardened hair. In fact it is made of cells that grow out from the surface skin of the nose. The cell tubules harden and fuse together. The horn is composed largely of the protein keratin, which is the same type of protein that makes up human hair and nails, horses' hooves and chickens' claws. Scientists and conservationists make a convincing case showing that rhino horn has little or no medicinal value. But as long as practitioners prescribe it and patients believe in it there will be a demand. Two thousand years of traditional medicine is even more convincing when backed up by an official's claim that it offers a miracle cure, and the news of it goes viral.

Today the world has rapidly dwindling wildlife resources and ever increasing demand from Southeast Asian markets for animal products to be used in traditional medicine. The rapid emergence of robust Asian economies is producing a consumer market that could prove the death knell for many species.

By early 2013 the value of rhino horn was $65,000 a kilo, which made it as valuable as many precious metals and the most expensive narcotics. The higher the value, the greater the risks people will take. Poachers know they risk being shot by armed rangers, and thieves are even prepared to poach horns from rhinos in zoos and from dead rhinos in museums. As Anthony Lawrence puts it in his book *The Last Rhinos*:

Shark-fin soup is no longer offered as widely on Chinese menus as it has been in the past.

'If you truly want to grasp the situation faced by conservationists, do what a poacher does and look at a rhino and see a 3ft-long horn made of pure gold. Game rangers are in the unenviable and extremely hazardous position of trying to protect solid gold. What should be locked securely in a vault instead walks around on four legs in the bush.'

Rhinos have been walking around in the bush for 50 million years but it's only in the last few years that they've been doing so with a lump of gold stuck on their heads!

Sharks are still being harvested at a rate that, for many species, is proving unsustainable. Ivory, lion bones, tiger body parts, rhino horns, and many other animal products are being gobbled up by countries who use them in medicine and as ornaments.

The ability of rhino horn or other animals' body parts to help with or cure human ailments may be a myth, but until the myth can be countered within the consumer markets, it will be responsible for the deaths of increasing numbers of threatened species and for their possible slide into extinction in the wild.

Drastic bid to save rhino

Melanie Gosling
Environment Writer

A WESTERN CAPE game reserve owner has resorted to desperate measures...

NEWS 5

'criminals' new ploy to obtain rhino horn

Tony Carnie

CRIMINAL syndicates have been roping in bogus sport-hunters from the Czech Republic, Poland and Russia to step around South Africa's ban on Vietnamese "people hunters" shooting rhinos and smuggling their horns to the East.

Last year, in an attempt to plug a legal loophole exploited by Vietnamese crime syndicates, Environment Minister Edna Molewa announced the government would not issue any more rhino-hunting permits to Vietnamese citizens.

Since 2003, Vietnamese nationals have hunted more than 400 rhinos legally in South Africa, sparking an outcry from conservation groups which pressured the

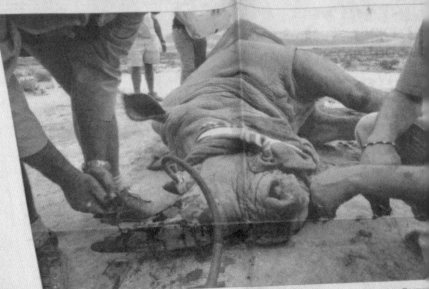

MEASURES: Wildlife vet Alex Lewis injects a mixture of dye and poison into the horn of this drugged rhino on Inverdoorn Game Reserve near Ceres. The oper... designed to deter poachers who are now targeting the Western Cape.

SA to propose legalising trade in rhino horn at Cites

Sipokazi Fokazi
Political Bureau

SOUTH AFRICA may legalise the trade in rhino horn if it convinces the international community to lift a ban on it.

Minister of Water and Environmental Affairs Edna Molewa said yesterday the country would propose a debate at the 16th meeting of the Convention on International Trade in Endangered Species (Cites), which begins on Sunday in Bangkok.

She would ask parties on the sidelines of the meeting to consider lifting the ban.

Her call comes amid soaring rates of rhino poaching, with about 600 rhinos killed and dehorned here last year.

Demand for rhino horn

WWF has said legalising the trade would increase poaching

including cancer.

Following the "Rhino Issues Management Process", which discussed funding rhino conservation, safety, security and trade, Molewa said the cabinet had been given recommendations which included establishing a national rhino fund and dehorning rhino.

would be required.

A study by her department had found dehorning would be a viable option only for small populations.

Molewa said while bigger voices, such as the World Wildlife Fund (WWF) and Kenya, had spoken out against legalising the rhino horn trade, the cabinet had to listen to other "smaller voices", mainly game farmers and rhino owners who were losing out due to the surge in poaching.

The WWF has said legalising the trade would increase poaching. WWF and Traffic would oppose any trade proposals at the Cites meeting. Kenya has called for a clean-up of the rhino-hunting industry

Runner bares all to raise rhino awareness

Zara Nicholson
Metro Writer

STARK naked except for a red rhino horn covering his proboscis, a Cape Town anti-poaching activist has mimicked the speeding Kloof Nek skater's video to raise awareness about the slaughter of rhinos.

Steve Newman, a gym manager, joined the "Spoofing the Kloof Nek Cam" bandwagon by doing a copycat video of Decio Lourenco's skating video which went viral earlier

this year 96 rhinos have been poached. Last year 668 were poached, and 448 in 2011.

So far this year 34 people have been arrested, while last year 267 people were arrested.

"We all live in this country and even if something doesn't affect your life directly, if we all change the way we think about things, we could make a big difference," Newman said.

He took the idea from Lourenco's video because of the instant popularity.

He said doing "something amusing" would get people talking and hopefully in helping the cause.

Newman aims to long lasting campaign funds for anti-projects. He is plann...

CHEEKY CAMPAIGN: A screen grab of Steve Newman's YouTube video of him running naked down Kloof Nek Road as part of his campaign to raise awareness about rhino poaching.

2 rhinos killed in sad start to 2013

Angelique Serrao

JOHANNESBURG: Two rhinos have been killed in the first week of the new year.

A five-day-old bull carcass was found on Saturday in the Madikwe Game Reserve in the North West. He was shot and both his horns removed...

11

The war against poaching

The phrase 'it's a war out there' is often used to
describe the struggle against rhino poaching. It's
an accurate description: weapons are being used,
armies are involved, and people are being killed.

In Chapter 9 we saw that past members of the British SAS, one of
the world's elite military units, were involved in Operation Lock in
the late 1980s and early 1990s. This was a covert operation set up to
gather intelligence about illegal rhino-horn trafficking.

Firearms and military personnel are not the only 'weapons'
deployed against poachers. Horns are worth poaching only because
of their high value. Making them valueless is an effective way of
protecting rhinos. In the mid-1980s Ed Hearn, the founder of the
Krugersdorp Lion & Rhino Nature Reserve, developed a procedure
to infuse the horns of rhinos with a pink dye and a pesticide. The
technique was later further developed, refined and then used by Alex
Lewis and Damien Vergnaud on the Inverdoorn Game Reserve in
2011 (see Chapter 6).

Obviously, infusing horns works as a deterrent only if it is known
that a specific animal or group of animals has been treated. Reserves
using this technique must therefore use every possible opportunity to
publicise its use on their rhinos. Promotional leaflets, signage at the

reserve, merchandise (T-shirts, etc.) and advertising must all carry the message: 'The horns of all our rhinos have been poisoned, coloured, and are X-ray detectable'. Reserves that follow this procedure could group together in an association and ensure that a list is published and widely distributed identifying those reserves with treated rhinos.

The horn-infusion procedure is not a foolproof cure for rhino poaching. There are those who claim that the dye and other ingredients disperse within months, but veterinary and scientific experts don't all agree; many think the potion remains indefinitely in the horns of fully mature animals. What is certainly true is that the treatment needs to be repeated every few years.

In places like the Kruger National Park where many animals are dispersed throughout a large area (the Kruger is the size of Israel), there would be issues not only with finding rhinos in order to treat them, but then permanently marking them as having been treated. It probably could be done, but it would be a huge and expensive operation that wouldn't alleviate the need for other measures such as anti-poaching ranger patrols. It is likely therefore that the infusion option will be of most use on relatively small reserves with limited numbers of rhinos.

Vergnaud, Lewis and others have set up 'The Rhino Protect Foundation'. It is completely independent of the Inverdoorn Game Reserve, and was created to pass on the expertise the Inverdoorn team has developed. The Foundation is talking to and working with a growing number of reserves including SANParks (Kruger and others), Sabi Sand, Gondwana, Garden Route, Timbavati and others who have already adopted this procedure, or are considering doing so. In the Sabi Sand Reserve, over 100 rhinos had been treated by early 2013. Sabi Sand used a combination of indelible dye and ectoparasiticides, and other reserves are experimenting with their own cocktails.

On reserves where the rhinos' horns have been infused, physical security has, in some cases, been reduced – but nowhere has it been abandoned altogether. This indicates that, for anti-poaching efforts to be effective, whether by private rhino owners or SANParks, a variety of strategies needs to be employed.

Darting rhinos and sawing off their horns has long been considered an effective option but it has several drawbacks. Darting, itself, can be a risky business as vet Alex Lewis has pointed out: in human medicine an anaesthetist carefully assesses patients before they are put to sleep to be operated on, whereas animals have no such assessments – the risk is consequently higher. Furthermore, when horns are removed in this way, their stubs remain and, with today's high rhino horn value, even these stubs can be worth the risk of killing a rhino.

Finally, horns do grow back so, like infusion, removal is not a permanent measure. However, another option is complete surgical removal of horns by vets, which could protect rhinos from poachers and safeguard a stock pool of breeding animals.

Armed anti-poaching patrols have limited effect, proven by the fact that although such patrols have increased each year, so has the number of rhinos being killed. In *Killing for Profit* Julian Rademeyer quotes Ken Maggs, the head of SANParks' Environmental Crime Investigation Unit (ECIS): 'Last year (2011) we killed twenty-one people. This year, it is about seven so far. Shooting people doesn't solve the problem at all. But you have to be aggressive.' Maggs commented further, 'All of the guys shot in the park have been in armed conflict. We can't just go and shoot somebody for the sake of shooting somebody. We are bound by laws, whereas the poachers are bound by no rules. A poacher can come in, see one of my guys and kill him. If he gets away with it, he gets away with it. These are armed aggressors coming across our border. Nobody asked a Mozambican to come across. At any one time there are ten to fifteen groups of poachers operating in the park in different areas, all armed with a multitude of weapons. They can come in a group of five, each armed with three weapons, and engage the rangers who – funnily enough – also have families and also live in communities and will be as sorely missed by their families and communities as the poachers are by theirs. We've had hundreds of thousands of people crossing the border from Mozambique into Kruger, and there is certainly no trend of us going out of our way to shoot people. The refugees who come through the park don't come through armed. So if you're coming through with an AK47, what exactly is it that you're wanting to do?'

As Maggs pointed out, soldiers, rangers and other government employees are bound by rules of engagement – whereas the poachers can do what they like. This means the criminals will always have the advantage as they can be proactive, while anti-poaching forces have to be reactive.

Drones are widely used in the war against terrorism, and armed drones often 'take out' their targets without the targets even knowing they have been identified. The use of drones or unmanned aerial vehicles (UAVs) for aerial reconnaissance in game parks is becoming more widespread, and is a more cost-efficient and effective way of patrolling large areas than are boots and wheels on the ground. Although drones used against wildlife poachers are armed only with cameras, the advantage is the same as with armed UAVs, i.e. the suspects often don't realise they have been sighted and filmed. However, if the drones identify suspicious activity, boots and wheels on the ground are still needed to intercept the suspects.

Rangers employed by the government (SANParks) and by private reserve owners find themselves on the front line of a real shooting war. They are heroes who are largely unsung: we salute them. The

On the Inverdoorn perimeter fence are clear warnings to poachers that the reserve's rhinos have all been treated, and so their horns are valueless.

Treating the horns with the triple-ingredient cocktail

high value of rhino horn has inevitably led to some corruption, and rangers have not been entirely exempt; but the majority of rangers and guides are dedicated to the welfare of the wildlife with which they work.

There are many who think the best way to protect rhinos is to stop or limit the illegal trade (poaching) by replacing it with legal trade. Rhinos can be farmed: horns can be removed from live captive animals, allowed to re-grow, and harvested again. Horns can also be removed from dead animals from both wild and captive stocks, and this could produce legal stockpiles of horns. Detractors believe that while increased supply from legal sources might depress values, it would only increase demand; those in favour argue that a carefully controlled legal supply of horn would undermine the illegal one.

Poachers' weapons: gun with anaesthetic darts

The legal trade in farmed crocodile skins is often used as an example of how legal trade can assist conservation. Ultimately, however, it comes back to supply and demand, and if the demand is big enough the supply can be both legal and illegal, and both can thrive as is evidenced by the trade in abalone and ivory.

The movement or translocation of animals to safer areas is another tactic used in the war against poaching. In mid-2013 six carefully selected rhinos were moved from the Phinda Private Game Reserve to Botswana where, after a quarantine period, they were released into the Okavango Delta. Poaching activity in Botswana is minimal, and it is hoped the animals will be safer there and will breed. In February 2014 South African conservationist Ian Player backed plans to move rhinos to Australia as part of a global effort to guard against their extinction. The Australian Rhino Project is led by former South African businessman Ray Dearlove and reflects growing concern over the future of rhinos.

The AK47 is a favourite weapon among poachers.

South Africa will host the next CITES meeting in 2016 and, according to Edna Molewa, the Environmental Affairs Minister, may present a case for being allowed to sell horn in a legal trade: 'Depending on the amount of thinking we will have done by 2016, we could put trade back on the agenda, or we could do it at the one thereafter in 2019. We can't take short cuts!'

The debate on how best to save the rhino is complex and the issues are many. While there are no simple, one-size-fits-all answers and no quick fixes, there are some certainties.

- If the present rate of increase in poaching continues, rhinos in the wild will once again be threatened with extinction.

- For CITES to be effective it needs to be given some teeth to punish member nations that transgress. The future and guardianship of the world's wild fauna and flora really should be in the hands of the UN or an international body set up by the UN, and given effective policing and sanction capabilities.

- To save the remaining wild rhinos we must utilise a combination of all the weapons in the armoury – armed anti-poaching patrols, aerial monitoring (drones), horn infusion, increased public awareness in consumer markets, a controlled legal supply, translocation to potentially safer places, and strict enforcement of internationally agreed measures. We must also work to curb – and ultimately stop – demand. If there is no demand for wildlife body parts, not only rhinos but also elephants, sharks, lions, tigers and many other animals will be safe, and mankind's conscience in this regard will be clear.

Save the rhino, hunt a poacher

We could save the rhino if we wanted to; the question is, will we?

International crime behind rhino losses

Man Friday
tony weaver

interpreter in rhino horn cas 'compromised'

WARDA MEYER

oung rhinos' tiny horn stumps did nothing to rotect them against sophisticated poaching gang

Charges against pair are likely to be reinstated

Crime, poaching means fees soar

From Page 1...

R1m reward offered for rhino poaching mastermind

JOHANNESBURG SANPark

Runner bares all to raise rhino awa

Zara Nicholson
Metro Writer

Reserve slammed for 'rhino hunt'

CHEEKY CAMPAIGN

UK rock musician Nick Burdett heard the
Higgins and Lady story and painted the cartoon above,
which he sent to the author as a present.

Epilogue

IN WRITING *THE POACHER'S MOON* I have tried to give readers a brief insight into the brutal world of rhino poaching in South Africa, a world driven by avarice and mistaken beliefs. But it is really the story of two rhinos, Higgins and Lady. Theirs should be a story of sunshine and fresh air, grazing, reproducing, and the natural cycles of life and death.

Instead, in 2011 their natural world collided with man's destructive, greed-fuelled way of life. For the rhinos the result of this clash was a new world of pain, blood, blindness, suffering and a mighty struggle to survive. Higgins' and Lady's scars have mostly healed now but the rhinos will be disfigured for life, and they have had to learn to live without their horn armoury.

Rhinos have lived on Earth for more than 50 million years compared to humans' span of less than half a million. If rhinos can survive the current poaching onslaught and hang on until Mother Nature strikes back, they may well still be around in another 50 million years, long after man has caused his own destruction.

But rhino poaching is just one of the many assaults on our world's ecosystems. Like humans, the world has to breathe. If we continue to rip out the Earth's lungs, which are the African and South American rainforests, we are moving down the path of disaster. While scientists debate whether climate change is man-made or part of a natural cycle, we continue on our largely unchecked rush to deplete the planet's natural resources, unmindful of the tipping point that looms ever closer.

I am writing this at Fairy Glen as I watch the rhinos in the distance going about their day. With time these mutilated rhinos have

Their trauma is past, and Higgins and Lady
may safely graze for the rest of their lives.

slowly regained some trust in humans. Higgins has allowed some
visitors, accompanied by someone he knows, to get quite close
before starting to snort, thus forcing them to back off. It seems as
if the sadness has gone. He gives the impression of having mostly
regained his sight, and his old boisterousness and protective
behaviour towards Lady has come back. Lady still seems more
nervous around vehicles and humans so perhaps her mental scars
are deeper.

I hope they are 'happy' again. Lady may even be harbouring a secret. She has been seen mating with Higgins, and only she knows whether she is pregnant; she may soon be able to raise a finger to the poachers and say 'You did your worst, but you couldn't destroy us; one day you'll be punished, but for the time being, we have won'.

In their little world, Higgins and Lady are unaware of what humans are doing to the planet; they have just had a paddle in the dam before going to lie down in the shade.

Acronyms

CITES	Convention on International Trade in Endangered Species of Wild Fauna & Flora
SANParks	South African National Parks
MOU	Memorandum of understanding
SAVA	South African Veterinary Association
SAS	Special Air Service
UAV	Unmanned aerial vehicle
WHO	World Health Organisation

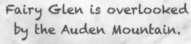

Fairy Glen is overlooked by the Auden Mountain.

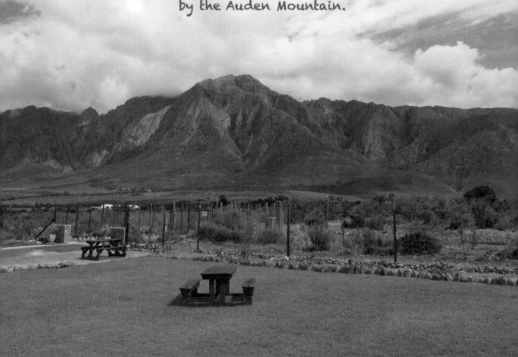

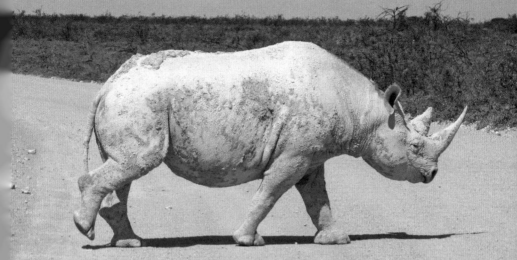

A black rhino in the wild

Useful websites

Adopt a Rhino	www.rhinos.org/adopt-a-rhino
Black Rhino Conservation Project	www.actforwildlife.org.uk
Born Free Foundation	www.bornfree.org.uk/
CITES	www.cites.org
International Rhino Foundation	www.rhinos.org
Project Rhino KZN	www.projectrhinokzn.org
Protect Rhino in South Africa	www.globalgiving.co.uk
The David Sheldrick Wildlife Trust	www.sheldrickwildlifetrust.org
Rhino Protect	www.rhinoprotect.org
South African Veterinary Association	
(Rhino Survivors Fund)	www.vetassociation.co.za/
Save the Rhino	www.savetherhino.org
Stop Rhino Poaching	www.stoprhinopoaching.com
TRAFFIC (the wildlife trade monitoring network)	www.traffic.org
World Wildlife Fund	www.wwf.org
The Endangered Wildlife Trust	www.ewt.org.za/Save-Our-Wildlife

Rhinos have lived on Earth for more than 50 million years compared to humans' span of less than half a million.